MIRACLES OF GRACE

MIRACLES OF GRACE

Edited and compiled by
Fr Frankie Mulgrew

NIHIL OBSTAT
Father Philip Caldwell STD
10th December 2017

IMPRIMATUR
John S.K. Arnold
Bishop of Salford
13th December 2017

ST PAULS by Westminster Cathedral
Morpeth Terrace, Victoria, London SW1P 1EP
Tel: +44 (0) 207 828 5582, www.stpauls.org.uk

ST PAULS Publishing
Moyglare Road, Maynooth, Co. Kildare, Ireland
Tel: +353 (1) 628 5933, www.stpauls.ie

Miracles of Grace is an abridgment of the original book, *Miracles R Us*,
published by St Pauls.

Miracles of Grace ISBN: 978-1-950939-00-8

Miracles R Us ISBN: 978-1-910365-39-7

Printed in Canada.

ST PAULS is an activity of the priests and brothers of the Society of St Paul
who proclaim the Gospel through the media of social communication.

To Mum
for teaching me to have faith
even in the darkest hour

'I can do all things through him
who strengthens me'
(Philippians 4:13)

CONTENTS

A Note on the Text

Quotations from Scripture are principally from the RSVCE. *YouCat* quotations are sometimes followed in square brackets by the number for the paragraph or paragraphs for which there is a correspondence in the *Catechism of the Catholic Church.*

CCC and *Catechism* stand for the *Catechism of the Catholic Church.*

TOB is an abbreviation of *Theology of the Body* by St Pope John Paul II.

Introduction

There is a guy I know who became a priest, but I met him even before he applied for the priesthood. We travelled together as part of a diocesan pilgrimage to World Youth Day in Sydney. At that time, I myself was training to be a priest, and we had profound conversations about the call to priesthood. This guy was from a rough neighbourhood, he was a former builder and was what some would call 'a man's man', so after he was accepted to train for the priesthood and before going to seminary he confessed that when he was first thinking about becoming a priest he worried he would never be good enough: 'But then I met (Fr) Frankie and I thought "If they're taking him they'll take anybody!"'

I love that story, because who am I that God would call me to be a priest? Thankfully, as that saying goes, God does not call the qualified, but qualifies the called. And who am I to edit and put together this book of amazing testimonies and reflections on God's love for us through the sacraments? (For those reading this book who may not be familiar with the Catholic faith, a sacrament is a physical sign or outward appearance of something miraculous that God is doing interiorly upon the soul, or – as the Church teaches – 'an outward sign of inward grace.') All sacraments have their roots and promises in Scripture. Bible expert Dr Scott Hahn explains that when Christ ascended to heaven He left us physically but He did not leave us spiritually, so all his power, love, and grace are available through the sacraments. In the Eucharist Christ is fully present as the ordinary bread and wine become his Body and Blood; in confession Christ is there through the priest; in the Sacrament of the Sick, Christ's healing is available.

So this book is going to talk about miracles – physical miracles, yes – but the greatest of miracles, the miracle upon the soul, a conversion of heart. Now I know that God does not always heal physically and I cannot say why some people receive physical healing whilst others do not. What I do know is that God always wants to perform miracles in the soul, which is the greater miracle to him, since our souls last for a million, trillion, billion years, for ever and ever, and our earthly bodies are temporary: they will be replaced by an immortal body on the Last Day (see 1 Corinthians 15:35-55). In the Gospels Jesus heals physically to show what He can do in our souls if we give him permission, and what we do now for our souls will have an effect for the good or the bad eternally.

An evident sign that the sacraments are working powerfully in our lives is the fruit they produce, as Jesus taught: 'You will know them by their fruit' (Matthew 7:16). It is great when we experience feelings and emotions through prayer, but it is not the be-all and end-all if we do not because, unlike our feelings and emotions, our souls are spiritual. The real sign that God is at work in us is the way our lives are transformed – for example, we want to pray more, receive the sacraments more, read the Scriptures more, be more compassionate, caring, stand up for social justice issues, and so on. Jesus said it is not feelings that save us, it is faith (see Luke 7:50).

Bishop Robert Barron reflects on how every sacrament is important for our lives: baptism puts God's divine life in us; confession restores that supernatural life when it is lost; the Eucharist feeds it, confirmation strengthens it, the Sacrament of Marriage and the Sacrament of Holy Orders give it vocational direction, and the Sacrament of the Anointing of the Sick heals it.

In this book, the chapters will not be going in the natural order of how a believer receives the sacraments during their life. The purpose of this book is to show the power and the miraculous that awaits you in each sacrament witnessed by our contributors at different stages/times of their life, but which inevitably began in their own baptism. And no doubt you will see in many cases how the different sacraments intersperse, infuse and complement the great work God has begun in someone through baptism.

So it is a great honour to compile all these great testimonies from very inspiring people who have profoundly experienced God's mercy through the sacraments. And if it has happened for them, it can happen for you!

THE SACRAMENT OF RECONCILIATION
(CONFESSION)

There is no saint without a past, no sinner without a future.

St Augustine

You can fly to heaven on the wings of confession and communion.

St John Bosco

Confession is an act of honesty and courage – an act of entrusting ourselves, beyond sin, to the mercy of a loving and forgiving God.

St Pope John Paul II

Confession Changed My Life

John Pridmore

My name is John Pridmore. I was born in the East End of London, England. When I was age 10, my parents told me to choose who I wanted to live with as they were getting divorced. I think this led me to make a decision inside myself not to love again, as the people you love just crush you.

By the age of 27 I had everything that the world says you need to be happy: a penthouse flat, sports cars, and more money than I could spend. The way I got my money was through organised crime. I was involved in major drug deals, protection rackets and violence of all kinds. I used to have a long leather jacket with a sewn-in pocket where I carried a machete. I tell you this not to glory in the past but to reveal the Glory of God.

One night I came home and was aware of a voice speaking to me inside my heart. I knew this voice was God's. At that moment, I said my first prayer and my life began to change. Unbeknown to me, my mother had prayed a novena to St Jude and it was the last day of the novena.

This led me to go on a retreat. My idea of a retreat was to be on a beach with a nice girl, a spliff and a whiskey. As you can imagine, it was not like I thought! The first talk was called 'Give me your wounded heart', and the priest said that each sin we commit is like a wound in our heart. As he was speaking I was looking at a crucifix and at that moment I knew why Jesus had died for me: He wanted me to be forgiven.

When I came out of the talk, I said a prayer to Our Blessed Mother Mary and asked her what Jesus wanted me to do. I felt her say, 'Go to confession.' I was afraid of what the priest might think, but Mary gave me the courage and I went to confession for over one hour. I was completely honest and did not leave anything out. Then the priest placed his hand on my head and gave me absolution, but it was not his hand, it was Christ's hand, and I knew in my heart that I was forgiven.

I did not know that our hearts are like a glass window: on one side is God's unconditional love pouring down every minute of every day, on the other side are all our sins, so we cannot see how much God loves us. We just see how unworthy of him we are, or even how worthless we are. I took all that sin and tipped it out at the foot of the cross and I was alive again: I could feel the wind on my face, I could hear the birds singing! Those sins had killed me inside, but confession had brought me back to life. When I looked at the priest's eyes, he was crying. He was not judging me, he was Jesus to me.

Now I live and work full-time for Jesus in St Patrick's Community based in Ireland. Many times I am asked by people, 'How do I personally meet Jesus?' I always answer, 'By going to confession and being completely honest.' He always comes to us in the humility of this wonderful sacrament of healing.

I now run a lot of parish missions around the world and at a mission in Derry, Northern Ireland, a man in his eighties came up to me, very emotional, thanking me. He said he had been going to Mass every Sunday since he was 7, but tonight he had met Jesus personally after going to confession for the first time in 48 years. At another mission in Tuam Cathedral a 15-year-old girl said, 'When you came to my school this morning I did not believe in God, but because of what you said, I came tonight, and because of what you said tonight, I went to confession. Not only do I know Jesus is real, but I know He loves me: confession has changed my life.'

Confession changed my life and I thank Jesus every day for the wonder of his mercy. I now go regularly and each time I feel like I am made new again in his love.

John Pridmore (UK) is an ex-London gangster, turned Catholic, who is now an international speaker and author with books including *From Gangland to Promised Land* and

Journey to Freedom. As a speaker he leads retreats, missions and conferences around the world, including speaking at World Youth Day in Sydney, 2008, before the Vigil service with Pope Benedict XVI. John's story has been featured on a number of secular television channels and in papers in the UK and Ireland.

Made for More

Leah Darrow

I was born and raised Catholic, but around 15 years old, I began to drift from the practice of my faith. I lost my virginity at 15 years old and unfortunately believed that because of my sins, I no longer had a place in the Catholic Church. I was scared Jesus wouldn't really forgive me and so I slowly did not practise my faith any more. I stopped receiving the sacraments and stopped believing that God would really make me happy. That's when I began to look to the world, to popular culture, to give me what I wanted.

I believed that to be somebody in this world I needed to be rich, famous and beautiful. This attitude led me to audition for the TV show *America's Next Top Model*. I was chosen to be on cycle 3 and this began my modelling career. After my time on *America's Next Top Model*, I decided to move to New York City and pursue modelling full time. I was able to get jobs on the runways in New York City with major clothing labels, and my picture was on the side of taxi cabs and on the billboards in NY Times Square. I thought all of this would make me happy. I thought making a lot of money, fame, and being told I was beautiful would make me feel successful and wanted. But none of these things made me feel happy, at peace or fulfilled. I was surprised that all of the fame, money and popularity ended up making me feel more alone and empty.

I always knew I was made for something great, and thought that my life as a professional model was that 'something great'. I received a phone call from an international magazine one day and they offered me a modelling job that would show people a different side to me. The magazine mentioned that I had always portrayed a nice, safe look but they thought I had something more to offer – that I could be sexy. I agreed to the photoshoot and thought it would help my career since the magazine is distributed all over the world.

On the day of the photoshoot, I was feeling irritated with my current life. My live-in boyfriend of two years said he loved me but didn't think we were ready for marriage, my party-lifestyle filled with drunken nights was getting old, and I began to question my purpose in life. I was tired of it all but still decided to show up for the magazine photoshoot.

As I got into hair and makeup, they wheeled in a rack of clothes for me to choose from. I did not feel comfortable with any of the outfits and it then became very clear to me that the 'more' they thought I had to offer was being a body to be objectified. I asked for a different set of clothing options to model but was informed that if I did not wear what they offered, I had to leave. I was scared and embarrassed, so I told them it was no problem, picked out a few outfits and the photoshoot began.

Halfway through the shoot, I accidently looked right into the flash from the camera. I asked for a few seconds to regain my focus. During the next few seconds, something happened that I did not expect or plan. As I blinked to regain my focus, I saw an image of myself inside my head – as if a little movie was playing. I was wearing the outfit that I was modelling; however, I had both hands cupped together at my waist which I then raised all the way up as if I was offering them to someone. At this time, I felt a massive feeling of disappointment, and so, brought my hands back down to see what was disappointing. As I looked into my hands, I saw nothing. Nothing. I had nothing to offer, nothing to give. A message was placed on my heart at this time that said to me, 'I made you for more.' I knew that this message was true. I *was* made for more than the life I was currently leading. God had given me so many gifts and talents, but I wasted them all on myself.

The photographer began snapping his fingers saying, 'Leah, focus. Let's get back to the shoot.' But I couldn't. Regardless of my past, I knew God was speaking to my heart and reminding me of my dignity and call to greatness. I told the photographer I had to leave and began walking toward the door. Before I walked out of the photo shoot, he said, 'If you leave, you'll be a nobody.' All I could say to him was, 'Do you promise?'

I had been away from the Catholic faith for over ten years and my sins and lifestyle were not bringing me peace. However, the reminder that I had been made for more and the promise of Revelations 21:5, 'Behold, I make all things new', was enough for me to give God another chance.

I knew I needed to change my life but felt overwhelmed with all of the choices of what to do first and how to do it. So, I began first with God. The one step I was sure of was Reconciliation. I needed to reconcile myself with God, to ask for forgiveness and the grace to live a better life. I had not been to the Sacrament of Reconciliation in years and was nervous. But I remembered, again, that I was made for more, and so I chose to go to confession immediately.

In that confession, I did not pretend to be a better person than I was; I was honest and gave Christ all of me. In return, Jesus gave me absolute and complete forgiveness, peace, joy and a new beginning. I believe Jesus was speaking to my heart during that photoshoot and He is right – We are made for more.

It is never a question of IF God will forgive you, it is only a question of WHEN – and we control the when. The mercy of Christ awaits all who seek it. I wish I had not been so selfish and prideful in my past so that I could have begun my journey with Christ sooner. But fear kept me from Christ. I beg all Christians: Do not allow fear to steal your joy and your place with Christ. 'We are not the sum of our weaknesses and failures, we are the sum of the Father's love for us and our real capacity to become the image of His Son Jesus' (St Pope John Paul II).

You have been made for more. I pray that you may experience the peace and joy of Christ's mercy and love. And remember, 'The world promises you comfort, but you were not made for comfort. You were made for greatness' (Pope Benedict XVI).

Leah Darrow (USA) is an international speaker, author and former contestant on *America's Next Top Model,* who travels all round the world with her message that truth, beauty and love are real and need reclaimed. Leah[1] has written her story in the book 'From Top Model to Role Model' and also proclaims this message through articles, podcasts and fashion tips available at https://leahdarrow.com.

---

1. The testimony contributed by Leah was originally written as a reflection for the Year of Mercy's '24 hours for the Lord' at the request of the Pontifical Council for the Promotion of the New Evangelization and is used by their kind permission.

Confession

Editor

A number of years back, before I was a priest, I was in my home parish church saying some prayers when a lady walked in whom I had never seen before. She was middle-aged with black hair, very pretty and well-dressed, but there seemed to be something bothering her. I couldn't help noticing her body language and her manner, so I approached her and asked, 'Is everything okay?' She responded, 'No.' Then she told me that for the past twenty years she had been an alcoholic and because of it she had wrecked two marriages, liquidated two businesses, and she was not even faithful to the person she was with at the moment. But most tragically of all, her two grown-up children now wanted nothing to do with her. She looked at me with desperation asking what she should do. I was not sure how to respond so I just shared with her about a time in my own life when I was struggling with depression but confession changed everything for me. I told her how I had experienced God's healing power, love and mercy in that sacrament and that it might have a similar effect on her.

She asked me when confession was available. I explained the time slots for Saturdays and she said she would think about coming back then. In an instant I knew this was a moment for the taking, that if she left today I may never see her again. I blurted out, 'But you could go to confession now if you want.' She said, 'What do you mean?'

I replied, 'I could run and get the priest next door and see if he would be willing to hear your confession.' She said, 'Let me think about it.' I replied that while she thought about it I would see if the priest was in. Running to the presbytery, I knocked on the door, and when the priest opened it I said, 'Father, there's a lady in there who is an alcoholic and has not gone to confession in over twenty years. Would you be willing to hear her confession?'

He agreed and prepared to go into the confessional. I went back to the church and explained to the lady that the priest was happy to hear her confession and that when the light went on outside of the confessional door that meant the priest was ready. He was ready to invite the mercy, forgiveness and power of God into her life, that this could really help her and be a true changing point.

> If you forgive the sins of any, they are forgiven them; if you retain the sins of any, they are retained.
>
> *John 20:23*

It was up to her. She was still unsure so I left her to it. The light outside the confessional went on and she got up and went in. I stayed outside praying. When she came out, although it was the same person, there was something different about her. It was like shackles had come off, she had been released from her chains and she was free and her body language and

27

manner showed it as she smiled. I suggested we say a short prayer together and then she left.

Fast-forward to about 18 months later. I was driving down the road in an area near the church and saw this same lady walking down the road… may I emphasise walking, not staggering! I pulled over and said, 'Remember me?' She did, so I offered her a lift, and as we were driving along I enquired how she had been. She said, 'Since that day in the church I have been to a clinic and dried out, but more importantly I am back in touch with my two grown-up children.' She went on to say, 'Things aren't perfect, but they're getting there.'

> God alone can forgive sins. Jesus could say 'Your sins are forgiven' (Mark 2:5) only because he is the Son of God. And priests can forgive sins in Jesus' place only because Jesus has given them that authority.
>
> *YouCat, 228 [1441-1442]*

I share that story for two reasons: first of all, to reveal the power of the Sacrament of Reconciliation; and secondly, to highlight the words of Jesus himself – the truth sets you free (John 8:32). God wants to heal our wounds and brokenness. But we need to step out of the darkness into the light. It is like going to the doctor's: a doctor cannot treat a disease you deny you have. But give the doctor specifics – a sore head, stomach ache, cannot lift my right arm – and he or she treats and prescribes accurately. It is exactly the same with God: He cannot treat any sins, mistakes, brokenness we have if we deny them and refuse to surrender them to him. There was a time in my life when I was really struggling with depression through OCD (Obsessive Compulsive Disorder) – in case you're not sure what that is, I'll give one example: I couldn't leave a place without making sure all the windows were shut, all the doors were locked and all the drawers were in. That may not sound like a big deal to you, but try checking out of a hotel! But a priest walked into my life at that time; it was an answer to a prayer, a priest I could trust with the darkness that was going in within me. I confided in him and he invited me to go to confession. I did not want to go, but I thought I had nothing to lose and everything to gain, so I did. I thought if I'm doing it, I'm doing it right; I need to get rid of everything that's on my heart. And at the end of this confession the priest put his hand over my head and said the words of absolution/forgiveness and as he was saying those words I felt this incredible breeze of heat literally rip through every core of my being interiorly – I had not known peace like it. And I knew God was there, helping me, pouring out his love and mercy.

Is God angry with me?

God is not some wrathful, vengeful God watching every move you make so He can notice every time you trip up. The reason God does not want us to sin is because when we do, we hurt those people closest to him – ourselves! Think about it: we are made in the image and likeness of God (Genesis 1:26-27), which means we're made to shimmer and shine, as Jesus said, to be a light to the world (Matthew 5:14). But when we sin we dent our own image of ourselves and then we can start to make the mistake of believing the lie that we are unlovable. God isn't angry with us. He loves us. He knows that sin separates us from the grace and love of our Father-God who wants to work so magnificently in us.

God just wants to take away your pain so you can be free

John Pridmore tells the story of getting a thorn stuck in his finger when he was a child. He did not want to show his mum, thinking she would pull it out and it would be very painful. So for three days he hid his finger from her, but eventually his finger was in that much pain he had to show her. Immediately she took out the thorn; his finger felt better and the healing process began. He thought to himself, 'What an idiot. I have been in pain these last three days and all my mum wanted to do is to take away the pain.' That is exactly the same with confession: all God wants to do is to take away our pain, reach into our hearts and remove the thorns that limit us and stop us from being free. Imagine if John had kept that thorn in his finger for months, even years—what would have happened to his finger and hand? Likewise, unconfessed sins that we carry around for years can become barriers and blockades to God's love and all he wants to give us, when he just wants us to be free. You deserve that love.

Who should go to confession?

According to St Paul, 'All have sinned and fall short of the glory of God' (Romans 3:23). He laments, in one of his letters, that the good he knows he should do, he doesn't do, and the bad he should never do, he does do (Romans 7:15-17). This also fits with the Scripture which says that even the just person sins seven times a day (Proverbs 24:16). But what is a serious sin?

I want to give an example of what the Church classifies as mortal/serious sin. This is when someone intentionally, with full knowledge and full consent, deliberately makes a decision to commit a grave offence (sin) – in other words, turning your back on God. Here's the thing: imagine standing in a river that comes up to your ankles. This river is meant to represent all God's love, mercy and power working in your life, which is not meant to stop at your ankles. It is meant to rise to your waist, to your shoulders, in fact to totally

> Three conditions are necessary for penance: contrition, which is sorrow for sin, together with a purpose of amendment; confession of sins without any omission; and satisfaction by means of good works.
>
> *St Thomas Aquinas*

consume you, so that God's divine love, mercy and power is in control, leading and guiding you. But imagine committing a mortal sin – like one of the Big Ten (the Ten Commandments – Exodus 20). The water evaporates and disperses until you are left with it just by your ankles: you are now struggling, trying, to live your life with limited grace. But confession restores the river and once again fills you with God's love, mercy and goodness. To put it another way (to take inspiration from Scott Hahn), it's like throwing the most amazing party in your heart with a joy and peace that cannot be matched. Serious sin, on the other hand, is like turning off the music, announcing there's no more dancing and ordering the Trinity out of your heart.

Your weaknesses do not define you and they certainly should not master you. If you haven't already, take hold of the chance to go to confession; it will change your life. And when you confess, get rid of everything! Confession is a real opportunity to be transformed. St Catherine of Siena believed going to confession is receiving 'baptism in the Spirit'. Even if you are not sure that God exists, go to confession and experience the mercy of a God who loved you so much He did not want to give you up without a fight.

Where can I receive God's mercy?

I have heard confessions in the most unusual places. Once at the Edinburgh Festival, when people spotted me with my priestly collar and assumed it was a costume, they kept asking, 'Which show are you in? Where's your venue?' I replied: 'Your local Catholic Church, once a day, twice on a Sunday, four-star reviews. I can get you front-row seats!' But one performer from the Festival who noticed my collar asked for confession.

On another occasion in Ireland I got a taxi to morning Mass. On the way to the church the taxi driver and I chatted socially about a number of issues, but faith was not mentioned. When we arrived at the church, with one foot on the tarmac and the other still in the car, I said to the taxi driver, 'I'll pray for you during Mass this morning.' He responded by saying, 'How does a person know if he's forgiven?'

I got back in the taxi and we had a conversation about God's inexpressible, unconditional love. After our chat, he asked me, 'Father, would you hear my confession?' And I said to this taxi driver, 'Certainly, but can you just turn off your meter otherwise it's going to cost me a fortune.' But seriously, God dished out his mercy to that man, who I'm sure when he

> Confession heals, confession justifies, confession grants pardon of sin, all hope consists in confession; in confession there is a chance for mercy.
>
> *St Isidore of Seville*

woke up that morning never expected God to impact his life in the way that he did that day.

Jesus showed his mercy to everyone and although He spent a significant amount of time in synagogues, He also was out and about: on top of hills, by lakesides, in the market squares, at dinner parties. His mercy was not limited to specific times and places but was for everyone.

Mercy on a Bus

I was fortunate to help in my diocese (the Diocese of Salford) with a project for the Year of Mercy: a Mercy Bus. Under the patronage of Bishop John Arnold, the concept was a double-decker bus specially designed with images of Pope Francis, priests hearing confession or giving a blessing, and so on, to advertise God's love and mercy. The Mercy Bus parked in town and city centres and shopping malls with priests on-board available for confession, blessings or just a chat. They were accompanied by young-adult volunteers who played live music and invited people on board. And if you came on board and paid a bus fare, after your confession we dropped you off at home. We didn't—I'm just kidding. One of the most inspiring things that resulted from this project was people returning to the Sacrament of Reconciliation after 10, 20, 30 years and having a profound encounter with God's mercy. Some said they were going to return to Mass. One man contacted our office and had a conversation with one of our group leaders, Lorraine. He said he had not been to confession in 20 years, that he didn't feel he could go to the Sacrament of Reconciliation in a church but that he was going to go that weekend on the Bus. Lorraine asked him what prompted his decision. He said, 'Because you are not waiting for me to come to you; you are coming out and meeting me where I am.' The visible outreach of the Bus was enough to encourage people to seek what they had previously been so afraid and reluctant to seek: God's unconditional mercy and love. I once heard a phrase: 'Sometimes you don't wait for your ship to sail in; you swim out to it.' Well, similarly, let's not wait for our Bus to pull up. Take the initiative and go to confession.

Why go to a priest in confession?

Because it is Jesus Christ who sends us priests, He is the one who gives the power and authority for them to be 'other Christs'. By merit of their ordination, when the bishop lays his hand on the heads of the priests, their souls ontologically change, for ever to conform to Christ's soul. So whenever a priest carries out ministry, he does so in the person of Christ himself. Therefore, in confession, it is Christ who reaches out and forgives and heals through the priest. What is

> Penance is the second baptism, the baptism of tears.
>
> *St Gregory Nazianzen*

said and confessed in this sacrament is between you and Christ: this is known as the seal of confession (see CCC 1467). A Catholic priest does not and cannot repeat any of what is said and confessed. If the priest repeated what was said and confessed, he would have his faculties/powers as a priest taken from him.

Sometimes I speak to people who believe they have done something so bad that they are too ashamed to confess it. But God's mercy is greater than the worst thing you have ever done, and we priests do not judge you when you come to confess. In fact, the more honest and upfront you are, the more a priest loves you and wants to reconcile you with God and the Church. I once asked a very holy man if there is one sin that cannot be forgiven. He said, 'Yes. Believing that nothing can be forgiven.' Think about it: God cannot give you anything you refuse to accept.

Let us take some case studies of God's mercy. Imagine if someone was a fraudster, a two-faced liar who manipulated people to get their way, cheating them of their money and possessions – could they be forgiven? Or what about a thief, someone who steals, hurts, judges and accuses others but does not see their own guilty deeds – could they be forgiven? Or what about an adulterer? Someone who has acted on selfish lust and pride with the marital act outside of marriage, causing deep pain and hurt – could they be forgiven? Well yes! Jesus forgave them all: they are

Zacchaeus the tax collector (Luke 19:1-10), the Good Thief (Luke 23:32-43) and the woman caught in adultery (John 8:1-11). They each experienced the mercy and loving presence of God, knew it was real and let him transform their lives: all by meeting a God who was ready to forgive.

> God esteems repentance so highly that the slightest repentance in the world, as long as it is genuine, causes him to forget any kind of sin, so that even the devils would have all their sins forgiven, if only they could have remorse.
>
> *St Francis de Sales*

There is only one condition: you have to want the mercy. God is a gentleman. He does not go where He is not invited. Everybody who encountered Christ in the Gospels all started out from a place of needing his mercy, and then they encountered him. The saints show us that God just doesn't want us to meet him once, but to continue encountering him and discovering more of his love and mercy for our lives. So, may I boldly suggest you receive this sacrament regularly?

We were born for greatness. When you go to confession and have been as honest as you could, when the priest puts his hand over your head (it's not his hand but Christ's hand) and you hear the words of absolution and forgiveness which the priest says over you at the end – in that moment your soul becomes as pure, as white, as beautiful and as ready for heaven as it was on the day of your baptism! God has raised his game. Are you ready to raise yours?

Our Lord Himself I saw in... this venerable
sacrament... I felt as if my chains fell, as those
of St Peter at the touch of the divine messenger.
My God, what new scenes for my soul.

St Elizabeth Ann Seton

Love covers over a multitude of sins.

1 Peter 4:8

It must be recalled that... this reconciliation with
God leads, as it were, to other reconciliations,
which repair the other breaches caused by sin.
The forgiven penitent is reconciled with himself in
his inmost being, where he regains his innermost
truth. He is reconciled with his brethren whom
he has in some way offended and wounded. He is
reconciled with the Church. He is reconciled with
all creation.

St Pope John Paul II

THE BLESSED SACRAMENT (EUCHARIST)

There is nothing so great, my children, as the Eucharist! Put all the good works in the world against one good Communion; they will be like a grain of dust beside a mountain.

St Jean Vianney

If when He lived in this world, He healed the sick by the mere touch of His garments, what doubt is there but that He will perform miracles, since He is so intimately within us, if we have a lively faith; and that He will grant us what we ask of Him, while He is in our house?

St Teresa of Avila

And they devoted themselves to the apostles' teaching and fellowship, to the breaking of bread and the prayers.

Acts 2:42

A Real Person

Sr Briege McKenna OSC

I am very aware that in the healing ministry God heals in a variety of ways: divine intervention through the sacraments, where God miraculously touches lives and heals them (a ministry that I'm called to with Fr Kevin Scallon); by giving us doctors, or people to help us find doctors; through medication. God works in all these ways to heal. Here I share with you a few true stories which I would call miracles of the Lord.

The first story was told to me by a mother who came to see me about a month ago:

> Sr Briege, she said, this happened quite a while back and I've never had a chance to tell you. You and Fr Kevin were ministering during a parish mission in the United States when my little boy was 9 years of age and had about 20 epileptic seizures a day. I was told that there would be a parish mission with a Eucharistic healing service so I brought little Nick. When Fr Kevin held up the monstrance you told the people, 'This is Jesus,' and reminded them what Jesus clearly told St Faustina: '"I'm not an object, I'm a living Person." This is the same Risen Jesus and I stress this.'

Well my little 9-year-old was really listening. He knew that every day he had to take all kinds of medication, he couldn't play soccer, he couldn't play any sports because of the disease. As he was listening to you he was also looking at Jesus in the monstrance; he was begging Jesus and I could see that it was affecting him in his faith. After the service we went home but he didn't say anything. The next morning when I had to give him his medicine he said, 'I don't want it.' I told him he had to take it as he couldn't go to school without it. He said, 'Mummy, no, because I'm healed. Last night Jesus was in the church and He told me I was healed when He was walking around.'

I looked at him and part of me was so scared and I asked, 'Are you sure?' He answered, 'But Mummy, do you not really believe that's Jesus? Because in the middle of the night He reminded me again.'

Today my son is an engineer and he has never had a seizure since that night at the parish mission. And he is completely changed.

The next miracle happened in a different way. A man who came to a mission we were giving was driving us to the airport afterwards and he told us his story:

A few years ago I was given a month to live, eaten away with cancer, no hope, when my friend said, 'You should come to a mission offered by Sr Briege and Fr Kevin. There's anointing for the sick and a healing service where they talk about the Eucharist.' I knew the mission was far away – two-and-a-half, three-hours travel – but I thought, well I'm dying and I'm going to be miserable anyway, so I might as well go. There were confessions the first night so I went to confession and then you prayed with me, Sr Briege. I had a wonderful encounter with Jesus in the Sacrament of Confession, attended the Eucharistic healing service afterwards and then went home. The next morning I got a phone call from the biggest pharmaceutical research company in America. I don't have a clue how they got my name but they said, 'Your name has been picked out with several other people who have radical cancer and no hope. Would you be willing to give us permission to experiment with a new drug which has just been brought out?' Something inside me said, 'That's why you went last night because I'm going to give you an avenue for healing.' Twenty of us cooperated with this treatment and I survived, completely healed through it, and I knew that it was because the Lord wanted to show that people who spend their lives trying to find cures for people through research are instruments of God. I was healed to give glory to God for the research of science and medicine because it completely eradicated my cancer.

People think of me as having a healing ministry but really it is through the sacraments of the Church that God heals. This is what I speak a lot about. Rarely have I been present when these miracles happen and that's the mercy of God because the Lord takes me away from the church or wherever we are ministering so the glory goes directly to the Lord and the sacraments.

Every sacrament is a door to Jesus. There are seven doors (and here I'm quoting Fr Kevin) and behind every door Jesus is waiting to minister to you. In baptism, the door opens for you to receive Jesus into your whole life so He can occupy your life, your soul, everything. In the Sacrament of Penance, you walk into the Jesus of Mercy; in Holy Communion you walk into Jesus the Bread of Life; in marriage you walk into Jesus who will unite your two hearts with his in the sacrament that makes him present. Holy Orders makes the priest so united to Jesus that he acts 'in the person of Christ'. People are looking all over for extraordinary things and this is why I tell Catholics, 'If you really believed, you would know that every single day the same Person who healed the blind man is in the church. If a doctor said, "Go and take chemotherapy because it's going to save your life," people would flock to the doctors. They believe the doctor, but they don't believe Jesus who said, "Come to me."'

The same with confession. The first extraordinary miracle that I saw from that sacrament was an unseen one, in the soul. In the western United States a man came to a mission looking for me to pray with his child but there was no 'praying with people' that night; it was the Sacrament of Reconciliation. He heard us speaking about confession and meeting Jesus and he went to confession. But because his reason for coming to the mission was to get me to pray, he left disappointed. This man, a bank manager, had a withered leg from polio. Two days after his confession his wife called Fr Kevin to tell him about her husband's leg: the muscle that had died through polio had started developing and by the end of the mission he had a perfect leg. By that time the whole bank had come to the mission!

Today I went to visit a priest who is dying. I told him never be afraid to ask the Lord for a miracle because you may not get physical healing, but you'll get even better: when you pray for miracles there's an opening to God who pours in his grace and that grace can either flood your body and physically heal you or it can flood your soul and prepare you for the Kingdom. It happens whether it's for this life or for the next.

Sr Briege McKenna OSC (Ireland) entered the Sisters of St Clare at the age of 15. She is known throughout the world for her healing and preaching ministry and ministry to priests along with Fr Kevin Scallon CM (Intercession for Priests). Sr Briege, who has travelled extensively around the world giving retreats and conferences, is also the author of *Miracles Do Happen*. She is the 2009 recipient of the Award for Outstanding Catholic Leadership from the Catholic Leadership Institute.

Healed from Fear

Emily Cavins

I have discovered there is enormous healing power in the Sacrament of the Eucharist. Several years ago, as I found myself tormented by a specific fear, I wondered how I could conquer this fear. I knew that the Eucharist was a sacrament that allows us to partake in the very life of Christ. I was familiar with the words in the Mass, 'Only say the word and I shall be healed' (now 'Only say the word and my soul shall be healed'). I decided these words definitely applied to my situation. During a Mass, as I approached the sacrament, I again prayed for Jesus to heal me. I did not feel anything out of the ordinary at that moment, but after that encounter with the living Christ, I experienced a change. It didn't happen all at once, but nevertheless there was a definite change for the better that continued until I was free of that fear. Many other factors came about in the healing process, but I feel those factors also came from the grace Christ gave me at that moment I received the sacrament. I was healed in much the same way as the centurion's servant in Matthew chapter 8. He received healing by Christ through those same words, 'Only say the word and my servant will be healed.' Those words of faith opened the doors of grace. You too can expectantly approach Jesus with your request for healing and he will answer you.

Emily Cavins (USA) is the author of *My Heart Is a Violin: The Autobiography of renowned violinist/composer and Holocaust Survivor Shony Alex Braun*. She is the developer of *Great Adventure Kids* Bible study materials that centre around teaching children the plan of salvation history based on her husband Jeff's *The Great Adventure: A Journey through the Bible*, available at Ascension Press. Emily and Jeff lead Scripture pilgrimages.

The High Priest's Promise for a Dying Man

Fr Leo E. Patalinghug IVDei

It was a busy day, typical for a young associate pastor trying to save the world. I was leaving from the hospital for my second call that day when I received yet another call to visit an elderly man in the nursing home. He was actively dying. His children were called to be with him in his last hours, or days. No one, but God, really knows those details.

I sprang into action, perhaps a bit too quickly – as a young enthusiastic priest. I called the family, all waiting at the bedside of their beloved father. I asked if he could receive Communion. They said they didn't know if he could swallow the Host. I should have presumed being prepared for Viaticum, just in case. But, being a bit too hasty, I didn't stop by the parish to obtain a reserved consecrated Host.

When I got to the nursing home, I met the charge nurse, a faithful parishioner. She knew and told me, 'Mr John was a very faithful parishioner who loved receiving the Eucharist. You can give him a very small piece and I'll melt ice to dissolve it so that he swallows it.'

I immediately felt bad for not bringing Holy Communion. I would have returned to the church to bring back Communion, but the family immediately invited me to the room for the anointing prayers. They were anxious too.

At the conclusion of the prayers, the dad was still unresponsive. I thought to myself, 'Maybe it was best not to bring Viaticum as he wouldn't know either way.' So, after a few consoling words, and before I was ready to depart, I invited the family to say an extra set of our Catholic 'Traditional-Trio' of prayers: the Our Father, Hail Mary and Glory Be. To our surprise, the father opened his eyes, looked at me and started to mouth the words slowly. I, myself, and the family around the bedside were shocked. We slowed down so that he could lead us (myself included) in the prayers. It was very touching indeed.

At the end of the prayers however, something strange happened. His eyes gazed upward, beyond us all. He then strained his neck and silently mouthed the word 'Amen'. He proceeded to open his mouth, put out his tongue, gently closed his mouth. He serenely closed his eyes and he softly began to chew. He then obviously swallowed 'something' satisfying because the look on his face was so serene.

I was shocked. My thoughts raced. 'Did he just receive Viaticum – Holy Communion? What was he chewing? Why did he say, "Amen" and look like he received Communion on the tongue? Did I just see a miracle? Did Jesus, the High Priest, give this man what I could not give him?'

I didn't see a mystical host, but we certainly witnessed something miraculous: an unresponsive dying man 'received' what appeared to be an invisible Holy Communion as Viaticum, more likely at the hands of the Divine Physician. We saw him chew and swallow something. We saw his peaceful expression, a definite sign that God was with him. After all, the word 'viaticum' simply means, *on the way with you*, to describe how the Eucharist, our Last Supper, is the Food on our journey to heaven. So, while I didn't bring Viaticum, that didn't stop God from accompanying this faithful man to everlasting life.

This experience, one that I will never forget, reminded me of how God can work through my limitations as a priest – even a young priest with boundless energy. My intention was good, my pastoral skills developing, and my desire to respond quickly was noble. But despite all of that, I wasn't prepared and didn't bring Holy Communion – something Mr John would have wanted. But, God answered his prayers, no thanks to me. Let's just say I'm grateful for my happy fault. It gave me a chance to experience something miraculous and to strengthen my faith that God is the one who initiates and completes the sacramental grace – even through the limitations of the priest.

This holy man died later that day. His family requested that I tell that story at the funeral homily. People received Communion in a more solemn fashion that day.

Viaticum *is* real. God *is* with us on our way to heaven. We can call it 'miraculous' that God would be so intimately united with us in our last days on earth to eternity. Or, we can just call it 'faith'.

Fr Leo E. Patalinghug (Philippines/USA) is a priest member of the community of consecrated life, Voluntas Dei (The Will of God). He is an international Author, Speaker, TV & Radio Host, and Founder of GraceBeforeMeals.com, an international apostolate to help strengthen families and relationship through God's gift of a family meal, and TheTableFoundation.org, whose mission is to elevate culture and family life, one meal at a time.

In that little host is the solution to all the problems of the world.

St Pope John Paul II

For I received from the Lord what I also delivered to you, that the Lord Jesus on the night when he was betrayed took bread, and when he had given thanks, he broke it, and said, 'This is my body, which is for you. Do this in remembrance of me.' In the same way also the chalice, after supper, saying, 'This chalice is the new covenant in my blood. Do this, as often as you drink it, in remembrance of me.'

1 Corinthians 11:23-25

There is no more effective way of drawing down God's blessing on a sinful, hungry, needy, wandering and confused world than by praying for others in Mass and through Mass.

Fr J. A. Hardon

THE SACRAMENT OF BAPTISM

Today your offences are blotted out and your names are written down. The priests blot out in the water, and Christ writes down in heaven.

St Ephraem the Syrian

We were buried therefore with him by baptism into death, so that as Christ was raised from the dead by the glory of the Father, we too might walk in newness of life.

Romans 6:4

And if [we are] children, then heirs, heirs of God and fellow heirs with Christ.

Romans 8:17

What Is God's Plan for Me?

Michael Dopp

I was 38 but unsure of many things. I didn't know what to make of St Boniface Catholic Church in Maryhill. While it was not my first time there, it was still new to me. The soaring ceilings, the deep red carpet, and the phenomenal high altar that held the remarkable statues of Jesus flanked by John the Evangelist and St Boniface – all inspired curiosity and awe.

Maryhill came about its name honestly. It is a village with deep German Catholic roots and so, when being renamed, the priest suggested it include the name of Mary. It is also a village with a striking hill on which sits the church. Thus these two characteristics were united to form the name of Maryhill. The parish was named after St Boniface, the tremendous missionary to Germany, who is remembered for cutting down a tree that was considered sacred by some Germanic pagans and building a Catholic Church out of it. He could wield both a Bible and an axe in his quest to become holy and to evangelise.

Many a tree was cut down to build St Boniface Church as it is a large and prominent building with a soaring steeple and magnificent stained glass. It was a suitable church as its size and presence echo the significant and vital change that was to happen to the trajectory of my life that day so many years ago.

My family – immediate and extended – gathered near the front although I was not sure why. I found out soon enough when, without warning, Fr Sherlock poured water upon my head and said, 'I baptise you in the name of the Father, and of the Son, and of the Holy Spirit.' I don't remember him saying these words, likely because I was only 38 days old. But I do know that he did say them, just as I know that those powerful words, prayed at the command of Christ, have welcomed the multitudes of the centuries into the Church.

It was the greatest day of my life. Yes. THE GREATEST. Born in the state of original sin and separation from God, my soul had been washed and cleansed. I was no longer in bondage to sin, but now enjoyed the freedom of a son of God. I became his child. The seed of grace that will grow, I hope, into the oak of glory was planted within me. I experienced the dying and rising with Christ of which Paul speaks. Where there was darkness in my soul, Christ brought his light. Where there was bondage, Christ brought freedom. Where there were the seeds of despair, Christ brought hope. And where there was a vacancy, God himself came to dwell. On 19 August 1979, I entered the Church. Like billions before me, my life was given a decisive shape and specific direction. I could echo the words of the martyrs in the moments before their death: I am a Christian.

But something else happened that day. I was given, in baptism, two missions: to be a saint and to be a missionary. I'll be straight with you: the call to heroic virtue/the perfection of charity/transforming union AND the call to share the Gospel of Jesus Christ with others – this can seem like quite a bit for a 38-day-old. I was just trying to not get spit-up on my white gown and to figure out how to use my fingers. Now I also had to be a saint and a missionary?

So here I am today. Still 38 but now *years* old rather than *days* old. Much has changed of course, but two fundamental truths remain as anchors for everything: I am still called to be a saint and I am still called to be a missionary. Now Christ, in his mercy, journeys with me in this. He feeds me with his sacraments, encourages me in prayer, and speaks in the silence of my heart. But since there is no specific and exact roadmap, the path I (and all of us) have taken has turns, valleys, detours, U-turns, potholes, red lights, breakdowns, oil leaks, empty tanks, and flat tires while also having gorgeous vistas, soaring mountains, quiet plains, bridges, and open roads. And what it has at the end of this long and singular path is simply him. God. He who came into my soul at baptism awaits me at the destination. He first came to live in me and to reveal to me his love. Now He invites me to heaven, where there is not a baptism but a marriage – the bridegroom and his Church. And He calls me to enter fully into this heavenly marriage now (holiness). But He also gives me the immense privilege of inviting others to this wedding feast (mission).

My life is ordered by, and to, these two vocations. It hasn't always worked out well. I am still far from the heights of holiness. And if I am poor at being a saint, I'm even poorer at being a missionary. Fear, pride, laziness, and a host of other sins and defects hold me back from being the missionary I am called to be. But Christ is patient. While He does not delight in my mediocrity, He sticks with me and continues to call me forth. His mercy is always available. He beckons me forward, reminding me that He will never ever ever ever give up on me.

And in my heart I do desire to respond. At times I feel like a pilgrim moving to the distant peak of a mountain. Up and down I go, climbing in heat and cold, going left, going right, trying to go straight. Then on occasions looking up. Sometimes it seems like the distant peak is not quite so distant. Sometimes it seems the distant peak is VERY distant. But one thing that cannot be denied – when I look behind I see the hills and valleys, rivers and meadows, the forests and fields that his grace has allowed me to cross.

God has brought me to a new place in these 38 years. I have grown a little in virtue, I am learning to pray, I try to evangelise. And anytime that I am off course, when the things of this world or the promises of the flesh or the lies of the devil ring in my ears, I can always be reminded of what God whispered to me at baptism: I was his son and by adoption, I was called to partake in his very life. This reorients my life. It reminds me and redirects me. It calls me back when I have wandered. But it also fills my heart with immense joy, for the path to the peak is a good path to a good peak.

It is a strange thing to peg an unremembered day as the greatest. Our baptism (as infants) has none of the nervousness of our first confession, excitement of our First Communion, anticipation of our confirmation, or outward celebrations of our wedding. It is a day like Nazareth – small, hidden, almost forgettable. Yet it is the day that really matters, for in it God gives us his dream for our life. So next time you wonder, 'What is God's plan for me?' remember that He told you already, sometime around when you were 38.

Michael Dopp (Canada) is the founder of the Mission of the Redeemer Ministries, The New Evangelization Summit and Relit, ministries that are involved with and dedicated to the New Evangelisation and training people up in evangelisation skills. Michael's ministry of speaking and teaching has taken him to evangelisation and mission projects in Europe, Africa, and North America.

The Gateway to Life in the Spirit

Michelle Moran

I grew up in a not very religious but loving and secure family. At the age of 16 my spiritual eyes were opened when I met members of a religious sect on the street in my home city. Thankfully, after this awakening, my search (or the Holy Spirit) led me to encountering the Lord in a personal way at a summer camp run by the Society of St Vincent de Paul. It was the early days of the Catholic Charismatic Renewal and many of the leaders at the camp were 'on fire' with the love of God. Their witness spoke so powerfully to me and I knew that I wanted whatever they had. So, to my surprise, at the end of my time at the camp, I found myself responding to an invitation to be prayed with. When I was asked what I wanted to receive from the Lord, my reply was 'everything'. The Lord always takes us at our word, so that initial conversion, which obviously needed to deepen and mature, has led me on a path whereby I have been a fulltime missionary for more than 30 years.

After the experience at the camp, I needed to enter into the community of the Church and it was a surprise for me to discover that I had been baptised as a baby and that baptism meant I was already part of the community. This was like encountering a previously undiscovered family; I now had a new sense of belonging. I learned that in baptism we are washed in the waters of regeneration and we are born anew. This is exactly what I had experienced at the camp. My life had been transformed and I now had a clear identity. I seemed to have more purpose and direction. Subsequently, I discovered that baptism is the most fundamental sacrament. It is the basis of the Christian life, the gateway to life in the Spirit and shared by all who call themselves Christian.

Over time I have come to see that baptism isn't just something done to us as infants. It is a stream of grace for daily living. In baptism, all the faithful are anointed as priests, prophets and kings. This anointing, together with confirmation, empowers me (and all the people of God) for ministry. I take my place alongside my brothers and sisters as part of the common priesthood, praying for the world. Baptismal grace helps us to radiate the love of God which has been poured into our hearts by the Holy Spirit (Romans 5:5). This profound witness of love can transform the world. Drawing upon the prophetic anointing of baptism enables me to trust in the Lord and find my voice, to not be afraid to speak words of truth and life. Sharing in Christ's kingship reminds me that I have a dignity and a role and responsibility within the body of Christ. However, Christ's kingship was not of this world. The call is to humble submission and to continue to embrace my baptism through dying to self in order to rise to new life. Undoubtedly, drawing upon my baptismal grace has been the bedrock and sustenance of my particular missionary calling over the past 30 years.

Michelle Moran (UK), together with her husband Peter, is a founder member of Sion Catholic Community for Evangelism in the UK. She has been engaged internationally in evangelism and mission fulltime for the past 30 years and has authored several books and articles about evangelisation. She is the former President of the International Catholic Charismatic Renewal Services, based in the Vatican, and she has been a member of the Pontifical Council for the Laity since 2008.

Plunged into New Life

Hannah Hayward

Baptism is best described, I think, as a kind of spiritual 'bath'. In fact, the word 'baptise' comes from the Greek word *baptizein* which means 'to plunge' or 'immerse'. The Church tells us that baptism is a sort of 'plunging' into Christ's burial and death, and a 'rising again' with Christ out of the grave into a 'new life'. This spiritual plunging is symbolised through three immersions (or pourings) of water. I may not have appreciated this apparently random soaking as a baby on the day of my baptism. However, now that I understand what it is to be truly clean, I am so grateful to my parents for ensuring I had a good wash, both spiritual and physical! In fact, the *Catechism of the Catholic Church* says that, at my baptism, I was 'freed from the power of darkness and brought into the realm of the freedom of the children of God' (CCC 1250). I love that description. What a wash!

However, I must admit, I can look at my own *spiritual* life and wonder 'Where did that purity go?' Where has that 'baptismal grace' gone in me? In baptism I know I was washed clean, I was filled with the life of Christ; but where has that life gone now? The answer, of course, is *nowhere*! I will always be baptised. It is not possible to be *un*baptised. The grace remains with me (unless I willingly sever myself completely from it through mortal sin). I am a child of God. Always. Unfortunately, the effects of sin remain, and I choose to reject this innate goodness and bathe in the muddy waters of self-determination, power-wielding, pride and greed. My 'grown-up' independence from God leads me away from his Fatherhood and into all kinds of dark and dangerous places. Every day, in small but definite ways, I turn from my baptismal identity as God's child and construct a different identity, independent from him. At worst, I actively defy him; at 'best' I simply forget He is even there. Either way, I often fail to *live* as I fundamentally *am*: a beloved child of God. In short, I sin. However, despite all this – and this is the grace of my baptism – Christ has placed his indelible mark on my soul, and it is Christ himself who, when I stray, tugs at my heart and brings me home.

I am realising now that my entire spiritual life boils down to experiencing more fully, more deeply, that 'supernatural childhood' that He gave me at baptism. Inevitably, this demands a surrender of heart, an admission to the fact that I have a Perfect Father to whom I can entrust my whole life. It means turning away from a life without God and back towards the loving arms of a Father who is totally reliable and totally loving. Baptism was the start of my journey to holiness. All the other sacraments are there to help me complete it! At confession, I am restored to that baptismal innocence. Through the Eucharist, I am again brought into that baptismal unity with Christ, but this time in the form of bread and wine. In my marriage, my soul is purified through a constant call to selfless love. I can easily be so unsure of my worth, and can find myself seeking the approval and honour of others. However, the Holy Spirit is a particularly good friend to me in this regard! I ask him, time and time again, to teach my heart more deeply of this knowledge of my true identity in Christ. At the start of each day, and in the face of any trial, I ask God's Holy Spirit to root me again in that foundational identity. It is the only foundation I have ever known to have never failed me!

Jared Harris, a recent graduate from Leeds Trinity University, passed through this initial sacramental threshold as an adult. His story speaks of the newness, liberation and belonging he felt when he was baptised:

I was baptised as an adult in 2014, whilst studying for a Theology degree at Leeds Trinity University. The sacrament had a great impact upon me then, and still has profound resonance for me today. What struck me most was the profession of faith and renouncing of evil, and the washing with water. During the profession of faith, I felt a great relief that what I had believed privately for a number of years could now finally be openly professed before the Church. My personal commitment to following God and rejecting evil was solemnly professed before the Church and my loved ones. It was not a new beginning in my faith journey, but my whole life in general. Through those baptismal waters, I truly felt I could let go of the sins and regrets of my past, and move forward. It is hard to explain the lightness I felt.

Although my problems didn't all disappear when I *was baptised* I felt that, with the Holy Spirit's help, I could now in a sense start again. I truly felt I had died with Christ to my old self and risen with him to a new life. It was real, and I had anticipated this moment for years. Being physically clothed with the white garment I felt, in a spiritual and material way, like I was beginning a new life. This personal conviction was confirmed when I proceeded, during the same Mass, to be confirmed and receive Jesus in Holy Communion. I also felt a deep bond with my Catholic friends as we could now receive the sacraments together; there was a great sense of community, which continues to this day.

In the weeks, months and years after that day I kept thinking back to what I had received, and it still has a deep impression on my soul. The trials of life did not disappear when I became a Christian, neither did my faults. In fact, there was a slight anti-climax when all the mundaneness of life carried on as usual as if nothing had changed. But deep down I know that something did change. On that day I became a child of God in a special way and through the help of his sacraments, I continue to become the person that God wills me to be.

Hannah Hayward (UK) is the Coordinating Lay Chaplain at Leeds Trinity University. She graduated from Leeds University in 2007 in Theology and International Development, BA, and worked as a Parish Youth Ministry Coordinator and Diocesan Youth Officer before taking up her current role. In 2012, she completed the Emmanuel School of Mission formation course in Rome.

For by one Spirit we were all baptised into one body – Jews or Greeks, slaves or free – and all were made to drink of one Spirit.

1 Corinthians 12:13

Through baptism each child is inserted into a gathering of friends who never abandon him in life or in death… This group of friends, this family of God, into which the child is now admitted, will always accompany him, even on days of suffering and in life's dark nights; it will give him consolation, comfort and light.

Pope Benedict XVI, 8 January 2006 (YouCat, Section Two)

Unless one is born of water and the Spirit, he cannot enter the Kingdom of God.

John 3:5

THE SACRAMENT OF MARRIAGE

The first natural tie of human society is man and wife.

St Augustine of Hippo

Love is patient and kind… Love does not insist on its own way… Love bears all things, believes all things, hopes all things, endures all things… Love never ends.

1 Corinthians 13:4-5, 7-8

'Authentic married love is caught up into divine love... so that this love may lead the spouses to God...' and in God they find the strength to carry on their roles and responsibilities.

Gaudium et Spes, 48

Making Dreams Become Reality

Chris Padgett

A few months ago, Linda and I started a married couple's ministry called The Bar (Building Authentic Relationships). The premise is simple: we find a neutral location that will put people at ease, provide some alcohol and get to know the people who come. At the midpoint of the meeting we all sit and I ask a question for each couple to answer individually, and then share with their spouse. If they are open, they can share with the rest of the group what they discussed. It has been an exciting time for all involved.

Last night's question was predicated upon the fact that everyone would have celebrated Christmas before we met again, so I asked them to reflect upon their first Christmas together as a couple, or possibly their favourite gift from their spouse. One couple decided to share their memory, but as they began he said, 'I won't tell you what I got for my wife last year, because she didn't use it.' She looked at him and asked, 'What did you get me that I didn't use?' He said, 'A tombstone.' We all about fell out of our chairs laughing. Till death do us part is certainly stated in most couple's vows, but buying a tombstone as a gift may be pushing things a little.

In 1987, I met a girl in high school who willingly went out on a first date with me – an unknown and awkward goofball whose claim to fame was winning the senior superlative: Most Unique Personality. We fell in love, and after a few years of dating we were married at the ripe old age of 21. This March, Linda and I will celebrate 25 years of marriage, and while it may be a cliché, I love her more today than I ever thought possible. So what tips can we offer on the Sacrament of Marriage?

There are three things I want to reflect upon when it comes to the importance of Catholic marriage. The first is the importance of growing together as a couple. The second addresses the necessity of being fully seen and learning to trust. And finally I will look at the joy of continuing to dream together.

As we begin, I first want to clarify a couple points. Catholicism says that marriage is a sacrament. There are necessary qualifications for this to be a sacramental marriage juxtaposed to a civil marriage, such as being free ecclesiastically, legally/societally and personally to marry, and being baptised Catholics. With each couple willingly entering into the lifelong commitment of marriage, the union reflects Jesus' love for his Church. He is the bridegroom and we the Church are the bride. The intimacy and union in marriage, which bespeak God's love, is tangible in the sacramental union. Christ is present, in a true way within marriage, to enable the couples the ability to bring one another to Heaven. In other words, men have one job in marriage: to get their wife to Heaven. Women have one job as well, and while it may be more difficult, they also are called to get their husband to Heaven. The mutual self-giving provides an avenue of true sacramental grace to bring about this goal. The journey will take a lifetime, but this is as it should be. Nothing of value accidentally happens, including a joyful and successful marriage.

Marriage was never to be reduced down to simply passion between one another, nor is it about finding common interests, or even mutual attraction. Marriage is meant to reflect God's love in time, and this is not predicated upon one's passions, attractions or even mutual areas of interest. Marriage is a holy opportunity to witness to one another and the world what real love looks like, over a long period of time. Yes, this love will have passion, and hopefully attraction and common interests, but it is durable, even when we get old and saggy, find ourselves interested in a variety of other things our spouse isn't keen on, and strong even when our eyes dim as our older selves fade into our final years. With that in mind, let's quickly look at three tips for growing in one's marriage.

The first area worth exploring is the need for each couple to willingly grow together throughout the years. I am not necessarily talking about body sizes, although let's face it, we all seem to expand over time, and as I've joked, while our bodies are temples of the Holy Spirit, I've been feeding mine like it is a Basilica! I remember hearing from my parents that one of the reasons their marriage didn't last was that they grew and became interested in different things that took them along different paths. This was always frustrating to me as a child, but even more so as an adult. Growing together, and finding peace in allowing one another to explore various new options, is something that is invaluable as a couple. You don't want to remain stagnant, so if one decides they want to try something new, I would advise doing this together. You will probably be stretched out of your comfort zone, but in the end it is worth being inconvenienced if it says to your spouse that you are willing to explore new avenues with them no matter what.

The second point is learning how to build a foundation of trust with your spouse. This happens when you quit pretending and trying to impress; rather, you allow your guard down and finally disclose who you are in all of its glory and mess. When a couple is together for a period of time, suddenly the truth of who each person is becomes quite clear. It is in the messy times that couples usually make a firm decision to either stick with one another or move on. In marriage, most couples have seen the good and the bad of their significant other. They accept these flaws and know God is at work. Over the years, couples recognise that while they still may be able to put on the charm at business meetings, or tell jokes that impress visiting friends, when everyone is gone and you are alone it isn't a joke or striking up the charisma that is needed in difficult moments. What is needed is authenticity. To love someone, even though they are broken and hurt, without excuse, and yet still be committed to them, I do believe that is where trust begins to thrive. In marriage, if you can have confidence that your spouse is with you in your place of authentic messiness, then you can breathe a sigh of relief knowing that a person is committed in our greatest and darkest hour. All marriages to really thrive need to be places of vulnerability and honesty.

Finally, the importance of a couple continuing to dream together cannot be overstated. I am amazed at how often couples seem to get lost in the regimented obligations and schedules of their daily tasks. Before they know it, the kids are out of school, out of the house and beginning their own lives. It is important for couples to continue to dream together, even during the busiest of times, so that they build into one another's life hope of a future together, even when the little ones are grown and gone. Linda and I have practised this habit of dreaming together with diligence. I would even be so bold as to say it is one of the things we love most about being married. Every year we make a little sheet of paper for each of the kids to tell what dreams they want to go after for that year. As a family we help each other's dreams to become realities. We do the same for us as a couple. The other day, Linda and I went through our little dream journal and we marked dates for all of the things we had accomplished over the years. Seeing all of those dreams come true was so inspiring. We spent a lot of time dreaming big for our future. I wonder if you could be brave enough to try and imagine what seemingly impossible things you could try this year, not worrying about money and time, age or distance; just dreaming about what you want and working to make it happen. That is one of the greatest joys of marriage: helping one another's dreams come true!

In the end, when I think of all of the times we have spent together as a couple, I realise I am a better man because of her. She is working hard at getting me to Heaven, and I have a feeling she may need to be around for a lot longer to make that a reality. I am hoping that's the case because we have some amazing dreams to bring to fruition.

Chris Padgett (USA) is an international speaker and musician, formerly of the Christian rock band Scarecrow and Tinman. Chris' ministries take him around the world doing concerts and keynotes, visiting parishes, conducting interviews and writing articles. Chris and his wife Linda Padgett live in Central New York, USA. You can read some of Linda's blogs at www.primalhappyplace.com and find out more about Chris and his ministry at www.chrispadgett. com.

What Do 'Soulmates' and Santa Claus Have in Common?

Jason Evert

When my parents broke the news to me that Santa Claus didn't exist, I stormed out of the room, blurting, 'I don't even want to know about the Easter Bunny!' Although the news was devastating at the time, I found solace in the fact I had obtained a more realistic grasp of how gifts arrived under our tree. Letting go of a childish notion of St Nick also paved the way for me to obtain a mature understanding of St Nicholas, the saintly bishop of the fourth century.

What does all of this have to do with finding 'the one'? Well, many people have a notion of soulmates that's in need of serious demythologising. In exchange, they can discover a mature Christian concept of their future (or current) spouse.

In his ancient text *The Symposium*, Plato presents the myth that men and women originally had four arms, four legs, and two faces. Unfortunately, Zeus split them in half as a punishment for their pride (which conveniently doubled his number of worshippers). Meanwhile, these incomplete individuals wandered the earth until they found their other halves. Upon discovering the other, the two would know they were made for one another, and would finally become whole.

Plato explains:

> After the division the two parts of man, each desiring his other half, came together, and throwing their arms about one another, entwined in mutual embraces, longing to grow into one, they were on the point of dying from hunger and self-neglect, because they did not like to do anything apart. (*The Symposium*)

Sounds more like Hollywood than Plato.

Looking for your better half? We should not expect another person to complete us. Let God do that. Some guys think, 'Since a wife is supposed to be your better half, I guess I'm only fifty per cent complete until I find her. When I find her, she will fill my emptiness and take care of all of my emotional needs.' If this guy finds a girl, it will not be a budding relationship; it will be a hostage situation.

Nevertheless, Hollywood has made a fortune perpetuating the eternal myth that there is a perfect person out there for each of us. But here's the problem: You're going to have to wait a lifetime before you can marry a perfect person. (For those familiar with the book of Revelation, I'm referring to the Wedding Feast of the Lamb.) Until then, anyone you marry is going to have his or her share of imperfections.

Sorry to be the bearer of bad news, but in this life, you're not going to find someone with whom you are perfectly compatible. After all, the word 'compatible' comes from the Latin *compati*, which means to 'suffer with' (*com* 'with', *pati* 'to suffer'). Successful marriages are not the result of finding a perfect person, but rather loving the imperfect person who you have chosen to marry. St Francis de Sales even described marriage as 'a perpetual exercise of mortification.'

Only God can complete us. When we make an idol out of a relationship, we are setting ourselves up for disappointment because all idols are meant to be broken.

Do soulmates exist?

If there's no perfect person made only for you, should we conclude from this that there's no heavenly plan for your love life? In a blog in which he makes many excellent points, Matt Walsh wrote, 'My wife and I weren't destined for each other. It wasn't fate that brought us together. We are bound not by karma, but by our choice.'[2] He goes on to say that God doesn't destine us to end up with anyone specific. Rather, there are countless people whom we could marry

---

2. http://www.theblaze.com/contributions/i-didnt-marry-the-one-she-become-the-one-after-i-married-her (last accessed 16 October 2017).

and be equally content. They become our soulmates when we marry them. We don't marry them because they are our soulmates.

While there is some merit to these ideas, the difficulty with this concept is that it doesn't leave much room for divine providence. For those theologians out there, it sounds more deist than theist. (Deism being the view that God exists, but that He is not directly involved in the world.)

In the book of Tobit, the archangel Raphael declares to Tobias, regarding his future wife, 'Do not be afraid, for *she was destined for you from eternity...* When Tobias heard these things, he fell in love with her and yearned deeply for her' (Tobit 6:17).

This isn't Hollywood; it's the Sacred Scriptures. We know Adam was made for Eve, Sarah was destined for Tobias, Joseph was created for Mary, and so on. But how, when, and why does God choose to play the role of a heavenly matchmaker?

Obviously, only God knows the answer to this. But we know that divine providence intervenes in our lives to the extent that we make room for it. Those who walk with God often marvel at how He seems to intervene in the most providential ways in the tiniest details of life. Believers routinely speak of 'divine appointments' and other occasions where we can see God's hand at work.

For example, Mother Teresa (St Teresa of Calcutta [Kolkata]) once said that a man came to her, seeking a specific medicine for his dying child. However, the drug could not be obtained in India. As she was speaking to the man, someone walked into the convent with a basket of half-used medicines. Right on top of the basket was the rare drug. She remarked:

> I just couldn't believe because if it was inside, I would not have seen it. If he had come before or after, I would not have connected. I just stood in front of that basket and kept looking at the bottle and in my mind I was saying, 'Millions and millions and millions of children in the world, how could God be concerned with that little child in the slums of Calcutta. To send that medicine, to send that man just at that time, to put that medicine right on the top and to send the full amount that the doctor had prescribed.' See how precious that little one was to God himself. How concerned He was for that little one.

If God is infinitely concerned with providing medicine to his children, you can rest assured He is also interested in providing for our vocations. I believe God the Father has a perfect plan for each of our lives, just as He had for his own Son. However, as Isaiah 55:9 tells us, 'For as the heavens are higher than the earth, so are my ways higher than your ways and my thoughts than your thoughts.' Sometimes this 'perfect' plan involves substantial suffering, but this does not make it any less perfect. Its perfection comes from the fact that it comes from the heart of a Father who loves us.

What this means is that God doesn't promise that you'll find the person who makes you the happiest, but if you remain open to his will, you'll discover the person who will make you the Holiest – and this will bring you more joy in the end than any plan you could have concocted without him. Your *soul* will be sanctified through this *mate*... and in my opinion, that's God's idea of blessing you with a soulmate.

Jason Evert (USA) is an international author and Chasity speaker who has founded Totus Tuus Press and the chastityproject.com. He has spoken on six continents about the virtue of chastity. He is the author of more than ten books, including *How to Find Your Soulmate without Losing Your Soul* and *Theology of the Body for Teens*. This and other reflections from him and the chastity project team can be found at: http://chastityproject.com/2015/03/soulmates-santa-claus-common/(last accessed September 2017).

Marriage, a Unique Sacrament

Marianne and Matthew Barnes

Marriage is a unique sacrament. It is the only sacrament that is shared between two people. Two people committing themselves with words spoken before God, words that echo through heaven, binding them for the rest of their lives on earth.

When I think about the moment I realised Matthew was 'the one', I find it difficult to pinpoint the exact time and place; rather, it was after a series of discussions I'd had with a holy woman and a holy man, a Carmelite nun behind bars (not prison bars obviously) and a priest during confession. It wasn't a lightning-bolt moment; it wasn't even anything Matthew did particularly that made me think 'Yep, that man's for keeps.' It was a series of open and honest heartfelt conversations with these particularly wise people that brought me to the knowledge that he was indeed my soulmate.

In my teenage years, I remember praying after receiving communion, 'Please, Lord, I'd rather be single for ever than have a rubbish man in my life' and I genuinely meant it. Maybe it was being the youngest of five and all my elder siblings having partners or husbands/wives at the time, but the concept of bringing a young man home to meet

my family filled me with utter dread. I was the baby—
they would undoubtedly poke fun at me and wind me up
something rotten—so at the time I met Matthew this was
not something I was looking forward to.

Matthew, on the other hand, could not wait to get into a
relationship. He tried to use prayer as a divine love potion:
'Please Lord make her fancy me, please Lord I want to marry
her, also can I have a Ferrari and a castle.' Thankfully God
laughed at his plans and Matthew soon realised it was
better to accept God's plan for him and started believing
in divine providence. He found that it was better to ask
God to help him realise what was best for him, rather than
using prayer as a wish list. He started to pray for help in
overcoming obstacles that were preventing him from being
the best version of himself. More importantly, he began
asking God to reveal his plan, whether it involved marriage,
the single life, priesthood or religious.

We met each other in Lourdes, travelling as youth
helpers. I was 17 and he was 18. He caught my attention
at the dinner table in the hotel where we were all staying,
not because of his dashing good looks and smart get-up.
No, in fact, he had shoulder-length greasy hair and was
wearing an old bobbly fleece. It was the way he held the
attention of every person around him and how they were
all hysterically laughing. I thought to myself, 'Oh he looks

like a laugh . . . I'll go and see what all the fun is about', only to find as soon as I sat down near him he blushed and went completely quiet.

We struck up an instant friendship and remained friends for a year, meeting at the planned reunions and nights out. The year after, we both went to World Youth Day in Cologne, Germany. This was a two-week trip which would start in Schoenstatt and end with Mass by Pope Benedict XVI in a field with over a million other young people. We drank German beer, sang Bavarian songs, danced on tables and talked and laughed. We really got to know each other and the spark was lit.

Our relationship developed further a few years later after we attended a reconciliation service at Our Lady's Shrine in Walsingham. The priest had asked me if I was considering marriage; he said that if I was serious about this relationship, it was important that we got to know each other spiritually and emotionally before getting to know each other physically. This gave me food for thought and when I shared this with Matthew, he told me that he was encouraged to write a prayer as his penance; so together we wrote a prayer, sat in a hayfield in Walsingham, and have continued to say it every day since. Even when we are apart this prayer brings us together:

Dear Lord,

Thank you for bringing us together,

Thank you for all the blessings you have bestowed upon
us, individually and as a couple,

We ask for your continued help and guidance, that we
may have a strong relationship now and forever,

Help us to grow together, spiritually, emotionally,
physically and psychologically

Help us to love each other, but above all help us to love,
together, our faith, our church and you our blessed
father.

Amen.

We dated for around five years before we got engaged and were married the year after.

Faith and spirituality has always been a big part of our relationship. We have always tried to encourage one another to deepen our knowledge and encounter Christ's spirit here on earth. We are blessed that we have had positive experiences and role models that have encouraged us to have faith. We have always tried to get involved with the Church where possible, whether this was volunteering our time for youth programmes or now just being part of the parish community. The purpose of marriage for me is building one another up so that you can be the best versions of yourself, who God wanted you to be.

We have both grown in confidence in our marriage, always knowing that we have the unwavering support and love of our partner. My prayer is that we will always love each other and continue to grow together in our marriage, and with God's help I know that we will.

Matthew and Marianne Barnes reside in the Diocese of Salford. They have been married six years and currently have two young sons. They are actively involved in their parish and wider community, in particular, leading marriage preparation and marriage enrichment courses and are members of the Diocesan Marriage and Family Life Committee, helping to bring the teachings of Pope Francis' encyclical *Amoris Laetitia* to all parishes within their Diocese.

Have you not read that he who made them from the beginning made them male and female... For this reason a man shall leave his father and mother and be joined to his wife, and the two shall become one. So they are no longer two but one. What therefore God has joined together, let no man put asunder.

Matthew 19:5-6

No one is without a family in this world: the Church is a home and family for everyone especially those who 'labour and are heavy laden.'

St Pope John Paul II

The family is, so to speak, the domestic Church. In it parents should, by their word and example, be the first preachers of the faith to their children.

Lumen Gentium, 11

THE SACRAMENT OF HOLY ORDERS
(PRIESTHOOD)

Priesthood is the love of the heart of Jesus.
When you see a priest, think of our Lord Jesus
Christ.

St John Vianney

Like living stones be yourselves built into a
spiritual house, to be a holy priesthood, to offer
spiritual sacrifices acceptable to God through
Jesus Christ.

1 Peter 2:5

The priest continues [Christ's] work of
redemption on earth.

St John Vianney

Discovering the 'More'

Christina Lynas

It was 5 April 2007, Holy Thursday. I sat in a small chapel in an old country house in the middle of the highlands of Scotland and it was the last place I wanted to be. My eldest sister had managed to talk me into going on retreat with her for the Easter Triduum and now I found myself with all these happy-clappy Christians who wanted to hug me. What had I got myself into?! Their joy and happiness annoyed me but I couldn't work out why... I believed in Jesus and went to church on Sundays but couldn't exactly call myself a good Catholic. I struggled with a lot of the teachings of the Church and had decided to live my faith on my own terms. For me the most important thing was to be nice and kind, so as long as I wasn't hurting other people then what was so wrong with the way I was living my life?

'Guilt, good old Catholic guilt. I am sure most of us know what that feels like.' The voice of the priest penetrated my daydream. Guilt. Yes, I knew all about that! I broke the rules, I felt guilty, I went to confession, I still felt guilty, I broke the rules again. This was the vicious circle of my life!

'This is NOT why Jesus came! This is NOT what Jesus wants for us!' Hmmm, the priest had my attention now...

'Jesus died, Jesus was tortured and freely embraced his cross, to wipe away all guilt! This is WHY Jesus came. Not to trap you in a life of guilt but to bring you to new life, a life of fullness, a life of TRUE freedom!'

I have no idea what else the priest or anyone else said to me the rest of that day, but these words had struck a chord with me and started whirring around in my head... So, is there another way?

The next morning – Good Friday – we were to climb a hill and pray the Stations of the Cross as we climbed. Before we climbed, one of the leaders said to me very gently and quietly, almost as if they were sharing a treasured secret with me, 'You know, if you had been the only one alive, Jesus still would have endured all his passion, just to save you. That is how much He loves you!' And off we went climbing up this steep hill with readings of his torture and pain echoing through my ears. 'Really, Lord?' my heart questioned. 'Do you really care about my life, about my sins? Was this for me?'

The answer to these questions came just hours later. We all gathered to watch *The Passion of the Christ*, a film I had never seen before, but I had heard the stories of how realistic it was. As I watched the love of Christ portrayed in each scene I was struck to the core, my heart moved with compassion and sorrow for all He endured. Then there was a moment, just as Jesus was carrying his cross, when He fell and looked directly at the screen. In this moment it was as if Christ was looking straight into my eyes, into my heart, and with such sorrow He whispered, 'This one was for you.' In an instant I knew that my sins **were** hurting someone. They were hurting Christ himself. Tears rolled down my cheeks and I wept through the end of the film. I now knew how desperately I needed to confess. Confessions were being heard in the next room and I rushed to join the short line.

As I walked in I was greeted with a warm and welcoming smile and then I began to confess. In my confession, I mentioned that I had said some of these sins before.

'Do you believe God has forgiven you?' the priest asked.

'I don't know,' was my reply.

'Do you believe He can?'

Again: 'I don't know.'

The priest challenged me with light and caring humour: 'Who are you, to say to God, "There's this one sin you can't or won't forgive."'

'Well, when you look at it like that...' I smiled.

'God has forgiven you all your sins; go in peace.' As I left, I **knew**, perhaps for the first time, that I was forgiven!

As my penance, I had to go into the chapel and lay my guilt down on the altar and leave it there, free myself of it. As I sat in this quiet chapel, I felt a deep sense of peace and then in the silence I felt the Lord speak to my heart: 'I want so much **more** for you than this.'

I knew these words to be a plea for me to change the way I was living, a plea from someone who loved me more than I could imagine, and I knew I had to try.

Ten years on I thank God for the profound grace of that confession, the truth that the priest spoke to me and the complete transformation that has taken place in my life. After that weekend I searched to know the Lord and our Church and to wrestle with all its teachings. The more I studied, the more I discovered the love and beauty that lies behind each one of these teachings. I have discovered the *more* that God wanted for me. This *more* is my living relationship with him, meeting with him in the sacraments, living in freedom of guilt and of fear, trusting in his great love for me and trusting in who He is: God Almighty, Creator of Heaven and Earth, my Father, my friend.

Thank you, Lord, for your love, your mercy and your priests!

The following passage is a constant reminder of the Father's love for me: Matthew 6:24-34:

> No one can serve two masters; for a slave will either hate the one and love the other, or be devoted to the one and despise the other. You cannot serve God and wealth. Therefore I tell you, do not worry about your life, what you will eat or what you will drink, or about your body, what you will wear. Is not life more than food, and the

body more than clothing? Look at the birds of the air; they neither sow nor reap nor gather into barns, and yet your heavenly Father feeds them. Are you not of more value than they? And can any of you by worrying add a single hour to your span of life? And why do you worry about clothing? Consider the lilies of the field, how they grow; they neither toil nor spin, yet I tell you, even Solomon in all his glory was not clothed like one of these. But if God so clothes the grass of the field, which is alive today and tomorrow is thrown into the oven, will he not much more clothe you – you of little faith? Therefore do not worry, saying, 'What will we eat?' or 'What will we drink?' or 'What will we wear?' For it is the Gentiles who strive for all these things; and indeed your heavenly Father knows that you need all these things. But strive first for the kingdom of God and his righteousness, and all these things will be given to you as well. So do not worry about tomorrow, for tomorrow will bring worries of its own. Today's trouble is enough for today.

Christina Lynas (UK) is the former managing director of Youth 2000, UK, who specialises in Youth Ministry and Mission; she was also a former member of the Craig Lodge Community, a retreat centre in Dalmally, Scotland.

One Miracle Every Day

Fr Lee Marshall

On a recent pilgrimage to Lourdes, a 15-year-old boy approached me after a Holy Hour of Adoration of the Blessed Sacrament – which it had been my privilege to lead. 'Father,' he said in a serious tone, 'I need to speak to you. Something happened to me during the Holy Hour!' I listened with wonder as he continued: 'As you exposed the Blessed Sacrament, I felt a heavy pressure pushing against my heart. Then I heard Jesus speak to me. The Lord asked me to follow him. In a vision I saw myself following Jesus… He turned towards me, showing his hands, and revealed that He desired me to become a priest.' At this point my young friend said he felt tears in his eyes. The strange force continued to press against his heart for the whole hour of prayer. Once the Blessed Sacrament was reposed, the pressure mysteriously lifted.

Encounters like this are not uncommon. The following day a young lady aged 16 approached me. She was beaming with joy. During that same Holy Hour she revealed that she had wept throughout, and described how through her tears, the pain she had felt inside for so long poured out of her. She had been full of joy ever since.

Strictly speaking, we might not define these two encounters as miraculous, but they are just two examples of the signs and wonders I have experienced week in, week out in my few short years as a priest. Catholics believe that Jesus is truly present in the Blessed Sacrament; He is no less present in the Mass than I am present – my body with its living blood flowing through my veins and of course the precious gift I carry, my soul. The Body of Christ, his Precious Blood and his Soul are also present in the Eucharist. This is truly awesome, but there's more, much more. His Divinity is also present: this means that Almighty God is present in the Eucharist! Is it any wonder that young men hear his call when they open their hearts and adore him? Is it any wonder that young women receive powerful inner healings in his presence? Of course not. The only wonder is that more people don't experience his presence in the Eucharist.

As a priest, I witness at least one miracle every day, at the moment I raise the bread and wine with my hands and they are no longer bread and wine, but the Body and Blood of Jesus Christ. One of the greatest joys of the priesthood occurs when the Lord reveals his miraculous presence in the Eucharist to those who it is my great privilege to serve.

After my young friend in Lourdes had finished recounting his testimony, I enquired, 'So how do you feel about becoming a priest?' He thought for a moment, then shrugged his shoulders, looked at me and said: 'It's not such a bad idea!'

Fr Lee Marshall (UK) is a priest for the Diocese of Hallam currently serving as Catholic Chaplain to Sheffield and Sheffield Hallam Universities. A regular homilist/speaker for Youth 2000 UK, he was formerly a financial director of a large architectural firm.

Priesthood

Editor with Fr Julian Green

In 2001, I felt God was calling me to the priesthood, so I applied. During this period, I said a prayer to Our Lady: 'If this is what your Son wants for me, send me a sign – a statue of yourself.' I thought that was a fair deal; I give my life to her Son and all she has to do is to produce one single statue. At the end of the year-long application process, I was not accepted. I went back to my career in show business.

Four years later I felt the call again, but this time door after door seemed to be opening for me to start my formation at seminary. I had forgotten that initial prayer all those years ago, but while attending a Catholic Conference, a lady I knew from Liverpool walked up to me and, pointing to a statue of Our Lady on the altar, asked me

> The government of souls is the art of arts.
>
> *St Gregory the Great*

if I liked it. 'Yes, I love it, it's beautiful,' I replied. 'That's my own personal statue. I lent it to the Conference for the weekend. People ask me if they can have it but I always say no.' Then she looked at me and said, 'Would you like it?' She didn't have to ask twice!

A short time later I was visiting my spiritual director. He said, 'Before we start today I want to show you something.' He brought me into a small room where there was a statue of Our Lady. Then he said, 'This was donated to the chaplaincy but I really feel you should have it.' Are you keeping count?! On the day of my Ordination, the Irish singer, Dana, and her husband, Damien, who are great friends of my family, presented me with a gift. It was a rectangular box, I shook it lightly, thought to myself could it really be? I took off the wrapping paper slowly, opened the lid of the box and guess what was inside the box? A statue – of St Anthony of Padua! I'm kidding. It was of Our Lady. That summer when I was on pilgrimage

> Thou art a priest for ever, after the order of Melchizedek.
>
> *Hebrews 7:17*

in Lourdes, I was sharing with a friend about the experience of receiving the first statue, then the second statue and then that third experience and she said, 'Well, that's Our Lady for you.' I said, 'What?' She said, 'That's Our Lady for you.' I said, 'What do you mean?' She said, 'Well, she's not once, not twice, but three times a Lady!'

Just as our earthly lives are formed in the wombs of our mothers and nurtured under their care, so are priestly vocations formed and nurtured under Our Lady's care. When people see a statue of Our Lady, they immediately think of Catholicism (even though she is the heavenly mother of all disciples). Sadly, when people want to attack the Catholic Church, it is often a statue of Our Lady they desecrate. This happened in the church in Mosul when terrorists brutally tore down a statue of Our Lady (which was later prayerfully reinstated when Iraqi soldiers from the Babylonian brigade rescued the city). Our Lady is recognised as Mother by all Catholics: Mother of the Church and Mother of us all. But for the priest, Mary is Mother in a particular way, for he sacramentally embodies her Son Jesus Christ, so he is related to the Mother of Christ in a more intimate way. In fact, the saints refer to the priest as 'another Christ'.

> Every baptised person is a member of the Priestly People of God and therefore represents Christ; and just as Jesus offered his life up to the Father on the cross, so we are all called to offer up our own lives to the Father. This is what is known as the 'common priesthood'. When a priest is ordained he does not stop being a member of this Priestly People of God, but his relationship to Jesus is intensified and acquires a new aspect. (*Lumen Gentium*, 11)

The priesthood – a new dimension

Jesus Christ is the one Mediator between God and men (1 Timothy 2:5). What is a mediator? When there is a dispute between two people, a mediator is the person who steps in between the two to try to draw them closer. Jesus Christ, however, is a greater Mediator than someone who just steps in between God and people to resolve the crisis of sin. Our faith proclaims that Jesus Christ is both true God and true man: He doesn't just step in-between; He himself is the reconciliation between God and humankind. Jesus' role as Mediator is seen most visibly when He hung upon the cross between heaven and earth. With his arms open He embraces the world, his head towards heaven and his feet towards earth, drawing all people to himself in order to bring them to his Father (John 12:32). He doesn't just offer himself to the Father; He brings all of us – with all of our sins, weaknesses, brokenness and vulnerability – through his own body into friendship with God.

That is what a priest does! His role is to draw people into deeper love and communion with God through his ministry and the sacraments: by baptising, celebrating Mass, hearing confessions, visiting the sick and dying, presiding at a wedding, conducting a funeral (and that can be all in a day's work – c'mon Spiderman and Ironman, keep up). The priest is invited to some of the most profound and important moments of a person's life to heal, bless, sanctify, redeem, as Jesus the High Priest works through him, despite the priest's own brokenness.

> Who then is the priest? He is the defender of truth, who stands with angels, gives glory with archangels, causes sacrifices to rise to the altar on high, shares Christ's priesthood, refashions creation, restores it in God's image, recreates it for the world on high and, even greater, is divinised and divinses.
>
> *St Gregory of Nazianzus*

One of my mentors was a Liverpool priest called Fr Jimmy Collins. He was a great influence on me because he was always ready to share God's light and mercy with others. He had an extraordinary healing ministry that packed churches and the Cathedral in the Liverpool Archdiocese. Everyone mattered to him as a unique, precious soul of God. He was a champion of the poor and vulnerable, helping them with both their spiritual and social needs. He was spiritual director of the Cursillo Movement in his area and author of spiritual books to open souls to God's grace. He was also a founding member of the Northern Catholic Conference, an event in the North of England, which has brought about great conversion of hearts and miracles. To me, his greatest attributes were his humility and great sense of humour in his service as a disciple of the Lord.

The essence of priesthood

The essence of priesthood is sacrifice! What makes Jesus different from the priests of the Old Testament is that rather than offering up an animal as a sacrifice to God for sins, Jesus offers his very self! And not only is He the priest who offers the sacrifice but He is also the victim: He himself is the sacrifice that takes away the sins of the world. When a man is ordained a priest in the Catholic Church he accepts the grace of God in the Sacrament of Holy Orders to become not just a priest but also a victim. Jesus is the only Mediator between God and man, but He gives the priest a share in his mediation, embracing the world and the effect of sin in the world. The priest will be there alongside people who are mourning, who are seeking forgiveness, who feel the burden of life with all the things that have been thrown at them. But he doesn't merely offer kind words and sympathy. Through his ministry he can raise up those people and unite them to new life, new hope in Christ, chiefly through the Mass and granting absolution in confession. On occasions such as being called to the bedside of a dying patient, who has been estranged from the Church for years, burdened with a serious sin, I realise in those moments God is saving a soul for all time and eternity.

The priest and the Mass

In the Mass, the priest isn't just a ceremonial host or a presenter, still less an entertainer. He stands in the place of Jesus, so that Jesus has a way of getting close to his people. The priest is clothed in vestments to show that he is not acting in his own name but in the Person of Jesus Christ the High Priest. He lends his voice, his hands, his whole self to Christ to offer the memorial of the one sacrifice of the Cross now made present. When the priest picks up the bread in his hands he does not say, 'This is Christ's Body,' but, 'This is my body.' He is lending his voice to Jesus. Repeating those words day after day the priest cannot help but realise that through Ordination Christ has made him someone who also has to give himself up for the good of the people. Just as a husband and a father hands over his life for the good of his family, so the priest united to Christ offers his life for the good of the Church. In celebrating the Mass the priest draws together all the cares, worries, problems of his people together with all of their joys, their hopes and their prayers, and unites them to the offering of Christ on Calvary.

A good example is Fr Walter Ciszek, an American Jesuit priest who smuggled himself into Communist Russia to serve God's people. In 1941, he was arrested by the Soviet secret police and spent 23 years in Stalin's prisons. Despite periods in solitary confinement, being beaten and starved, he served his fellow prisoners by saying Mass for them and offering confession, even though he knew that, if he was caught, he would face death.

> Priestly ordination is administered as a means of salvation, not for an individual man, but rather for the whole Church.
>
> *St Thomas Aquinas*

Greater works than Jesus?

Scott Hahn reflects on what Jesus meant when He said to his disciples that they 'will perform even greater works' than He did (John 14:12). One may ask, 'How is that possible? Think of the great miracles and signs Christ was responsible for!' But these are the words of Jesus himself, which means they must be true.

So how exactly would the apostles perform greater works?

They would perform baptism, which is a greater work than creation itself. They would forgive sins, which, as St Augustine said, is a greater work than raising the dead. They would celebrate Mass, which brings heaven into the midst of the world. These are divine actions. These are the greater works, and there are no greater works than these. It is for these, the sacraments, that Jesus ordained his priests.[3]

In the privacy and intimacy of the confessional, the priest will come across all sorts of human sins, some rather 'every day' sins, others more serious, but he doesn't hear those confessions of sin out of interest or to acquire information. He hears them so he can unite those sins and the sinner to the Cross of Christ. In the challenging words of Archbishop Fulton Sheen, when the priest holds out his hand and says the words of absolution it is as if his fingers are dripping with the blood of Christ. And when the priest says, 'I absolve you from your sins,' we are taken back to the Upper Room where Jesus appeared to his disciples and breathed his Holy Spirit upon them saying, 'If you forgive the sins of any, they are forgiven' (John 20:23).

---

3. Hahn, Scott, *Many Are Called* (Doubleday Religion, 2010, New York), p. 136.

That same power and authority which Jesus gave the apostles is given to every priest at his Ordination through the 'laying on of hands' by the Bishop. People share all sorts of problems and quite intimate details with each other when they trust one another, but the priest just isn't hearing the sins of the penitent because he is a trustworthy person or can give some good advice. Those who come to confess their sins do so with a firm conviction that this man has been changed into one who mediates and distributes the forgiveness and mercy of God: it is Christ acting through him. For example, when an angel sees a priest saying Mass they do not see the priest, they see Christ. When an angel sees a priest hearing confessions, they do not see the priest, but Christ, as is the case in all sacraments they administer.

> As for the proud minister, he is to be ranked with the devil. Christ's gift is not thereby profaned: what flows through Him keeps its purity, and what passes through him remains clear and reaches the fertile earth… The spiritual power of the sacrament is indeed comparable to light: those to be enlightened receive it in its purity, and if it should pass through defiled beings, it is not itself defiled.
>
> *St Augustine*

On the fateful night of 14 April 1912, when the Titanic was sinking, Fr Thomas Byles, a priest on board, was given two opportunities to get into a lifeboat. Instead, Fr Byles chose to hear confessions and counsel those who were about to die. Accounts say he gathered people of all religions together for prayers and even baptised passengers. His place was with the people, God's people, hearing their confessions and giving them forgiveness and absolution as the ship was going down, heroically sacrificing himself to prepare them to meet their Maker.

Why does a priest give up marriage?

So, this all sounds great, but why does the Catholic Church say that most of its priests should give up the hope of marriage and family life in order to be a priest? The clue is in what we have already said about the complete self-giving of Christ on the Cross for the sake of his Body the Church. A man on his wedding day takes a solemn vow to give his life entirely for the sake of his bride and for the family that they will have. This is a natural desire for every man. Some people will say that it is unnatural to expect a man to sacrifice this desire. That's true – it isn't natural, it's supernatural! Jesus said it is a gift granted to some – not to everyone – adding: 'Let anyone accept this who can' (Mt 19:11-12).

> God said: They are My anointed ones, and I call them My Christs, because I have given them the office of administering Me to you, and have placed them like fragrant flowers in the mystical body of holy Church. The angel himself has no such dignity, for I have given it to those men whom I have chosen for my ministers, and whom I have appointed as earthly angels in this life.
>
> *St Catherine of Siena*

On his Ordination day, the priest accepts not only a share in Christ's priesthood but also a share in Christ's marriage to his Bride the Church. The love which a man would show for his wife and children becomes the priest's dedication and devotedness to the Church. And let's understand the Church here not as an institution, but as the real people he dedicates and gives up his life for in his ministry — the members of Christ's Body. St Pope John Paul II described the priest as 'a man for others'. What he celebrates at the Mass he lives in his daily life, as he is blessed, broken and shared out for God's people.

A Catholic priest who administers the sacraments acts not on the basis of his own power or moral perfection (which unfortunately he often lacks), but rather 'in persona Christi'. Through his ordination, the transforming, healing, saving power of Christ is grafted onto him. Because a priest has nothing of his own, he is above all a servant. The distinguishing characteristic of every authentic priest, therefore, is humble astonishment at his own vocation.

YouCat, 250

That our Lord was descended from Judah . . . becomes even more evident when another priest arises in the likeness of Melchizedek, who has become a priest, not according to a legal requirement concerning bodily descent but by the power of an indestructible life.

Hebrews 7:14-16

Let everyone be struck with fear, the whole world tremble, and the heavens exult when Christ, the Son of the living God, is present on the altar in the hands of a priest!

St Francis of Assisi

THE SACRAMENT OF CONFIRMATION

God's love has been poured into our hearts through the Holy Spirit who has been given to us.

Romans 5:5

In the Old Testament, the People of God expected the outpouring of the Holy Spirit upon the Messiah. Jesus lived his life in a special Spirit of love and of perfect unity with his Father in heaven. This Spirit of Jesus was the 'Holy Spirit' for whom the people of Israel longed; this was the same Spirit whom Jesus promised to his disciples, the same Spirit who descended upon the disciples fifty days after Easter, on the feast of Pentecost. And it is again this same Holy Spirit of Jesus who descends upon everyone who receives the Sacrament of Confirmation.

YouCat, 204

It is better to be a child of God than king of the whole world.

St Aloysius Gonzaga

Shining Light of Faith

Chris Stefanick

Thanks to my parents I always had a sense of God's presence and as a little kid I wanted to be a saint. The roots they gave me never fully withered, though I came dangerously close to destroying them during the insanity known as 'junior high'.

I remember once in the sixth grade I was coloring at a friend's house after school with a crayon in one hand and a shot of Jack Daniel's in the other. By the seventh grade the crayons had disappeared and the world took centre stage in my heart. I was on an IV-drip of toxic music and my highest aspirations, like those of my rock gods, were to obtain alcohol, party and mess around with girls. I wanted to be famous. I wanted to be a great guitarist. I wanted to be drunk. I wanted pleasure. I wanted a lot of things that had absolutely nothing to do with Church!

Thanks be to God, He rescued me before I became a train wreck. When I was going into eighth grade, my parents dragged me off to a retreat that changed my life. I felt new life pulsing through the dying faith-roots that had been planted in me as a young child.

It wasn't just the keynotes or the prayer experiences at this conference that changed me. It was the faces of the attendees that left an indelible mark on my soul. They had something I had been looking for in all the wrong places. I wanted what they had! The early Christians referred to themselves simply as 'the living ones'. I had been dead and I wanted to be among the living again.

And I experienced joy – real joy. Not the 'pleasure' I got from my misguided pursuits, but something weightier – something that would still be there when I was sober. Real joy is the soul's response to an overwhelming outpouring of Love. It's what you get when you find God and realise your purpose in life. But that realisation didn't fully 'stick' in my life until I started living it out and sharing it with others, and the Sacrament of Confirmation helped me do that mightily.

In general, grace isn't something we 'feel'. We can smell flowers, taste burgers, shiver from a cold wind, but grace isn't physical, so sometimes it's not even accompanied by strong feelings – but we can know it's there because Jesus told us so. When we feel it, that's a gift to us, often to teach us something or to strengthen us. When we don't feel any consolation in prayer or from sacraments, God's asking us not to get caught up in emotion, to deepen in faith, and to prove our love for him by seeking him for his own sake, not just for the positive feelings faith can bring. All that being stated, God let me feel the grace when I was confirmed.

I remember when the bishop anointed my forehead. As he pulled his thumb away from my head I felt the grace hit me like a ton of bricks. I remember it distinctly because it wasn't a feeling I've had any other time before or since. It was the sense of getting hit with an enormous zap of power. I didn't want to laugh. I didn't want to cry. I just stood there speechless. I was supposed to say 'Amen' in response to his words, 'Be sealed with the Holy Spirit', but I could barely utter a sound.

The months after I received that sacrament I noticed an undeniable change in the way I lived out my Catholic faith. The happiness, love, purpose, and peace I had from my faith became contagious. In my junior year of high school, I made it my goal to share my faith or a Saint story with one person per day. 'Give me someone to tell about you, Lord' was my constant prayer. I helped to start a prayer and faith sharing group, recruited people to youth ministry at my parish, godfathered a peer who was baptised, stood up for the dignity of women in the locker room, stood by those being mocked, went to pro-life marches, and, by the grace of God, I did it all in a way that was strangely 'cool'. Picture a longhaired teen guitarist in the 90s with baggy shorts talking to potheads about Jesus, with a rosary hanging from his belt. That was me.

My faith was no longer hidden from the world in the 'Upper Room' of my heart. I wore it on my shirtsleeve.

And I was remembered by faculty and students years after I left high school for being a witness. I had been a shining light of faith.

It's been my goal to keep shining that light ever since... to be like the LIVING ONES who changed my life as a kid – and more, it's my goal to help others be the same. We have the best news ever. We can't keep it to ourselves.

Chris Stefanick (USA) is an international speaker, author and founder of reallifecatholic.com. Real Life Catholic's purpose is to ignite a bold, contagious faith in the heart of every Catholic in America, through media and live events. Chris' books include *Absolute Relativism* and *Joy to the World*. This story originally appeared in *Chosen: Your Journey through Confirmation*, which is an award-winning Confirmation programme for parishes available at AscensionPress.com.

The Healing Power of God Today

Kristina Cooper

As a journalist, I can be a bit sceptical when I hear stories of healing. Are people really healed or is it just a rush of emotion brought on by being in a crowd at a big event? But I have had sufficient personal experience over the last thirty years or so to know that God really does heal today.

My first experience of healing was when I worked as a volunteer in a children's home in Panama City when I was in my late twenties. Linda, the cook in the home, was a godly Christian woman, but she could also be very short-tempered and at times unreasonable. There had been one of her periodic blowouts and there was a lot of tension in the home. In an effort to make peace, my friend Lydia and I went down to the kitchen to chat with her. She told us that she was very upset because she had been to the doctors recently and had been told that she needed a cataract operation otherwise she would go blind. She was devastated as she had been saving up to go and visit her son in America. Now it seemed all her money would need to go on this operation. We really felt for her, but it was more out of a sense of compassion and friendship than anything else that we offered to pray for her. I can't even remember if we asked God to heal her; we just prayed for her. A few days later I went down to the kitchen and found Linda in a fantastic mood. She told me that she had been to the doctor again. It seemed she was healed and now she didn't need an operation after all! I was shocked. I certainly hadn't had faith for this, but she accepted it quite naturally. I remember telling a fellow journalist about this some years later. She wanted to know if I had the paperwork and concrete evidence to back this story up. But I don't. When these things happen in your everyday life, you don't think about proving it, because the evidence is before you.

In the same way I believe that there are many such healings going on all around us through God's action and the power of the Holy Spirit. These are usually only known among a person's network of friends and family. They have no interest in having an officially recognised healing as such. They are just glad to get their health and their life back. The stories I now tell are these kinds of healings. They have not been rigorously investigated or researched, but I know they are true because I have been part of the story or have interviewed the person concerned and seen the evidence in their life.

Roberto, one good friend of mine, has had several healings over the course of his remarkable life. A former boxing champion, he suffered brain damage as a result of the blows he received in the ring. When he was in his twenties he was suddenly struck down, and for a year lay in a hospital bed with locked-in syndrome. He could hear and see, but he couldn't move or speak. The doctors said he would never talk or walk again and would be a permanent invalid. His mother, a devout Orthodox Christian, went to Corfu where she came from. Here she prayed at the tomb of St Spiridon, the patron saint of the island, who was known to be a great intercessor for healing and miracles. She was a simple woman, but she had a close relationship with Jesus and trusted him implicitly, believing that God would hear her petition for her son. We, in the secular West, can sometimes dismiss these examples of popular religiosity but the Lord sees the heart and the charism of faith behind them, and her prayers were answered.

Shortly afterwards, Roberto, for the first time, started to respond to the therapy that he was being given. The doctors were unable to explain why this was happening, as clinically this should have been impossible. This was not an instant healing, but one which involved years of painstaking therapy and rehabilitation as Roberto learnt to walk and talk again. Thirty years later Roberto, although he is still registered disabled, is able to lead a more or less normal life. The doctors have no explanation of why this has been possible as MRI scans show that his condition has not changed.

Roberto's physical healing also went alongside a religious and moral conversion too. In his former life, he was involved in a lot of criminal activity, but in the year 1999, following a deep encounter with Jesus, he returned to the practice of his Catholic faith in a very committed way. In gratitude for all that God has done for him, he feels called to live a life of service to the Church and the wider community. He is very aware that it is God who has healed him and him alone who sustains him. Thus he avails himself of all the sacraments that the Church has to offer on a regular basis. He receives the Eucharist daily, goes to confession once a week and receives the sacrament of the sick at a monthly healing service in his parish at St Mary's in Croydon. He also has received deliverance prayer on several occasions from priests involved in this often little-understood ministry. This has helped to deliver him from the negative spiritual effects of the dark forces in which he was involved in his past life of violence as well as alcoholism and drug addiction. This ministry, he says, has helped bring him great emotional freedom and spiritual liberation.

As if this was not enough, the Lord has continued to perform other significant healings in his life, which I have been witness to. One was about seven years ago, when he came to help me to man a stall at a Catholic Miracle Rally in London organised by the Cor et Lumen Christi community. Roberto shouldn't really have been there because he was in great pain with his knee, which was badly swollen and inflamed. He had recently been to the doctor to have his knee syringed of blood and fluid and his GP had decided that surgery was now needed to remedy the situation. This had happened with his other knee, some years previously. A date was thus set for a few weeks later at the local hospital.

We had been busy over the lunch break and were about to go off and eat, when I suggested to Roberto that we pop into the hall for a short while to see what was going on. Damian Stayne, who was leading the service, was praying for an outpouring of the Holy Spirit. Many people in the hall were speaking in tongues, which is a special prayer language mentioned in the Bible. As I work for the Charismatic Renewal, this was something quite commonplace for me, and after ten minutes or so, as I was hungry, I suggested that we leave and go and have a cup of tea. Roberto didn't say anything at the time. Later, however, he told me that he had felt very dizzy as people had prayed, and he had felt the power of the Holy Spirit strongly in the room. It was only the next day that he realised he had no more pain in his knee and that he could bend it and walk on it as normal again.

He decided he would still attend his hospital appointment to witness to his healing to the doctors and tell them that he didn't need the operation any more. Rather than dismissing what he said, it turned out that both doctors were women of faith. One was a Christian and the other a Muslim. They both rejoiced with him, saying 'God can do anything He wants,' without insisting on taking another X-ray or going ahead with the operation. All I can say is that seven years later I can testify that Roberto's knee is still fine.

Kristina Cooper (UK) is a speaker, journalist and editor of *GoodNews Magazine*, a magazine for Catholic Charismatic Renewal (CCR) in the UK and Ireland, a resource for those who are keen to grow in their spiritual journey.

Fanning into Flames the Gifts and Sacraments

Ros Powell

I was speaking at Waterford in Southern Ireland. It was a weekend for leaders and people who attended local prayer groups. I prayed with this couple and they'd just received the baptism in the Holy Spirit. They asked me if I would pray especially for their young daughter. I think she was about 15, 16, something like that.

I really felt on my heart to say to them, 'Well instead of praying for, could I pray with? Could you bring her tomorrow?' My faith levels were high, so I said, 'If you bring her tomorrow God will heal her.' They told me that she had been born with a birth defect and over the next couple of weeks she had to go into the hospital for a corrective operation. She had one leg shorter than the other which threw her hip out and she couldn't walk properly. They said, 'Oh, I don't think she'll come because she's away from the Mass; she doesn't believe so much in God like she used to when she was little.'

The next morning she walked into the meeting with her parents. I went over to her and I said, 'Can we pray?' I felt the Holy Spirit was saying to me, 'Just pray for healing for her, don't mention to her about going back to the Mass, or the sacraments.' I was just led by the Holy Spirit; we went into an adjoining room and the parents said to me, 'Do you want us to go out?' And I said 'No, I need you to help me in prayer.'

When I prayed for them the day before for the baptism in the Holy Spirit they had both received the gift of tongues. The girl sat down and I did as I had been told and just spoke about healing. I didn't mention to her about coming back to the Lord. Her parents helped me by praying in tongues over her legs. I measured her legs and one leg was much shorter than the other. As I laid my hands on her I could feel the shorter leg moving and growing; I could feel the leg shooting out from the hip sockets as we prayed in tongues for maybe about ten minutes. I asked her, 'How are you?' She said, 'I am fine.' I said, 'Stand up.' She stood up, and she said, 'Wow that's amazing.'

I asked, 'What percentage do you think you're healed?' And she said, 'About ninety per cent.' So I said, 'Okay, let's pray again.' We prayed again, and again she stood up. I said, 'What percentage are you healed?' And she said, 'A hundred per cent.' The shorter leg had grown to the same size as the other one. She could now walk normally without a limp. All of us were crying because Jesus had healed her, which meant that she wouldn't need to go into the hospital to have an operation. As the day went on I noticed that she stayed on and attended Mass, which was beautiful. The Lord then released me to talk to her about the Holy

Mass. After Mass I went over to her and asked if I could pray with her for the baptism in the Holy Spirit. She said, 'Yes please.' So I prayed for the baptism in the Holy Spirit and she came back to God, which of course was the greater healing of the two.

Our Church was birthed at Pentecost when the Holy Spirit came in the form of tongues of fire and rested upon the 120 in the Upper Room including Mary the Mother of Jesus. The first gift that they received was the fire, then the next gift that they received was a gift of praying in tongues. Peter – who previously had denied the Lord three times – was changed from a jellyfish to a rock. God gave Peter great boldness. And on that following day when they went into the market place, people actually thought that they were drunk. They were drunk in the power of the Holy Spirit, and Peter brought 3000 converts to the Lord. They had been baptised in the Holy Spirit.

I usually say to people when I pray with them for the baptism in the Holy Spirit, 'Let's fan into flames your infant baptism and your Confirmation. Everything's already there but sometimes if we are backslidden we have to "fan it into flames and ignite it again" (2 Timothy 1:6).' I know with me when I first received the baptism of the Holy Spirit I felt like a Hoover cleaner (everything is there but in order for it to work it needs plugging into the electricity supply).

I had been baptised and confirmed but I needed to be plugging into God's electricity supply, which happened for me when someone laid their hands on me (Acts 8:17; 19:5-6; 28:8).

And the Lord ignited all the sacraments I had received the way He did at Pentecost – the Lord Jesus when He was Ascending up to heaven said I will leave you the comforter (John 14:16) and we all need that comforter (Holy Spirit); when you love someone you just don't tell them once that you love them. If you're besotted with them you keep on telling them that you love them. YOU KEEP ON FANNING THE FLAME.

I have a prison ministry; I found that God gave me a gift of great boldness when I was baptised in the Holy Spirit and the doors of the prison ministry opened up to me. What I find is that when we go into the prisons the Lord gives me such great boldness when I'm speaking to really hardened criminals. I tell them about how God loves sinners; I tell them that God loves to forgive even the vilest sinners. I tell them about Mary Magdalene who had seven demons cast out of her (Luke 8:2); I mention to them about the thief on the cross and on that day he was going to be with the Lord in paradise (Luke 23:39-43).

When I go into the prisons I take three men with me that who have served time in prison. They give their testimony and then we say to the lads or the girls, do you want to surrender to Jesus? I would then take them through a prayer where they surrender to Jesus and ask the Holy Spirit to come into their lives. After that we would pray over them individually – Oh! We see miracles; we just see so many miracles! Out of the inmates we speak to, we have an 80 per cent response: 80 per cent of them get baptised in the Holy Spirit and receive the gift of tongues. It's wonderful.

We went to a Category B prison recently (Category B would be the long-term serious-crime inmates). The punishment system they have in this particular prison we were visiting is what's known as 'lock-up' (they are placed in solitary confinement). The last time we went there, four lads were in lock-up, isolated away from the other lads because of unruly behaviour. They are usually highly guarded. On this particular time, I miraculously got permission to go into lock-up and minister to the four lads that were in there. I was able to see them individually in their separate rooms and all four gave their life to Jesus and all four spoke in tongues. You come away and go wow! Wow! Thank you, Jesus, for setting them free.

Ros Powell (UK) is a speaker with a healing and prison ministry. She speaks regularly at conferences, seminars, and retreats and regularly ministers in prisons. She is a member of the English National Service Committee (NSC), the principal coordinating organisation of the

Catholic Charismatic Renewal (CCR) in England. She is also Spiritual Director to Precious Life – the largest pro-life group in the North of Ireland.

Led by the Hand of God

Jeff Cavins

I grew up in the 60s and 70s when the Catholic Church was experiencing dramatic changes after Vatican II. By the time I reached the age of confirmation, I was woefully lacking in the basic understanding of the faith. I do however recall that day in May of 1971 when I was confirmed and received a Bible as a gift. I was intrigued by this gift and held it in awe, figuring at some point in my life I would try to understand it. My brilliant idea was to read one verse a day in hopes of finishing it when I was old with a full understanding of the holy book. My plan only lasted a few weeks, however. The Bible remained on my bed stand for a few years until we moved to a new house several miles away.

Five years later, inspired by a Protestant family that read the Bible a lot, I bought a leather Bible and began to read it with great excitement. Over the years, that led me to teaching the Bible Timeline, a method of understanding the Scriptures by following 14 narratives in the books of the Bible that follow the story of salvation. Eventually I developed several Bible study courses. One evening while I was attending a volunteers' thank-you dinner for small group leaders of a local Bible study that I had been teaching, I mentioned to the group that I would be leading a pilgrimage to the Holy Land and for those interested, I sent around a sheet of paper. When the paper made the rounds and returned to my table, the gentleman next to me jotted down his address.

I couldn't believe it! He lived in my boyhood home! 'My parents built that house!' I exclaimed. Then I asked him if he wouldn't mind if I came to his house to see it. He was very generous and offered for the whole family to visit, including my parents and sisters. A few rooms still had the decorations my mother had made. I asked if he wouldn't mind if I saw my old room.

'Sure,' he replied. 'Which room is it?'

'It's the first one down the hall to the left,' I said pointing.

'Oh, that room is now my office,' he said, leading us all down the hall.

As I peered into that familiar room, I gasped. There, where my bed stand used to be holding my confirmation Bible, now stood a whole display case with all of the Bible studies I had produced. We were all amazed.

I was so blessed to see the tangible results of the anointing of the Holy Spirit at confirmation. That drawing by the Holy Spirit to read the Bible, which began at confirmation, grew into a library of studies now sitting on a shelf in the same location.

Jeff Cavins (USA) is an international speaker and creator of *The Great Adventure: A Journey through the Bible* – a practical, useful, interactive Bible timeline system currently being used in parishes across North America. For six years, Jeff produced and hosted EWTN's *Life on the Rock* and is currently the host of Relevant Radio's drive-time show *Morning Air.* Jeff is also the editor and writer of Catholic Scripture Study along with Scott Hahn, Mark Shea and others, available weekly at CatholicExchange.com.

Now when the apostles at Jerusalem heard that
Samaria had received the word of God, they sent to
them Peter and John, who came down and prayed
for them that they might receive the Holy Spirit;
for the Spirit had not yet fallen on any of them,
but they had only been baptised in the name of the
Lord Jesus.

Acts 8:14-16

And when Paul had laid his hands upon them, the
Holy Spirit came on them; and they spoke with
tongues and prophesied.

Acts 19:6

It is not in our power not to feel or to forget an
offence; but the heart that offers itself to the Holy
Spirit turns injury into compassion and purifies the
memory in transforming the hurt into intercession.

CCC 2843

THE SACRAMENT OF THE ANOINTING
OF THE SICK

This was to fulfil what was spoken by the prophet Isaiah, 'He took our infirmities and bore our diseases.'

Matthew 8:17

[In my name] they will lay their hands on the sick, and they will recover.

Mark 16:18

For I am the Lord, your healer.

Exodus 15:26

'I can pray too'

Fr Timothy Radcliffe OP

One day, some thirty years ago, I was sitting in my room in Blackfriars, Oxford, when the phone rang. It was a friend of mine ringing from the hospital, telling me that her 18-year-old son, John, had jumped out of the window of a flat on the seventh floor of an apartment block in London in an attempted suicide. I offered to come to the hospital but she said that there was no need since he would soon be dead. I decided to go anyway, since she and her husband would be in deep distress.

John was a charming, sensitive and intelligent young man, artistic and spiritual. But he had been caught taking drugs at his boarding school and been expelled. This had plunged him into a dark hole. His parents decided to take him on a trip around Africa to ease his pain. His mother had gone to collect the plane tickets but on the way back she found a crowd gathered in the road, and in the middle there was her son, his body broken. In the hospital they found that he had damaged most of his internal organs, and was not, it seemed, long for this world.

When I arrived in the hospital, to my surprise he was still just alive. The doctor told me that his core temperature was dropping and that he would die soon. I anointed him

139

and whispered, 'John, I am here. We are praying for you.' Somehow he managed to scribble a tiny note in spidery letters, 'I can pray too.' I still have the note. Then his temperature stopped dropping, and slowly death receded. It seemed like a miracle. His recovery took months. I visited him in the hospital. He was stretched out on a silk net, like a crucified man. I had to lie on the floor and look up to talk to him.

Two things struck me. His suffering was, in a way, a symptom of his goodness, his sensitivity. Secondly, I felt that the sacrament somehow blessed his inner strength and goodness. St Thomas Aquinas said that grace perfects nature and does not destroy it. Somehow, it seemed that God's strong grace reached down and vitalised the forces of life within him, releasing its self-healing power. God works at the very core of our being, where his grace and our strength are one. John is now married and has a child.

Fr Timothy Radcliffe OP is a priest and Dominican Friar. He was the Master of the Dominican Order from 1992 to 2001. He is the author of spiritual and religious books, and the winner of the 2007 Michael Ramsey prize for theological writing for his book *What Is the Point of Being a Christian?* He travels extensively throughout the world giving retreats, lecturing and speaking at conferences.

'Wait, He's Going to Respond to the Sacrament'

Sr Helena Burns FSP

I am telling this story second-hand, but it's such an extraordinary illustration of **God working through matter** (another name for the sacraments) that it has vividly stuck with me through the years.

A good friend of mine, Hannah Carter, was at the bedside of her dying father who was in hospice in a city far from where she lived. Hannah didn't know any of the priests in the area, so she called a local parish to ask for the Sacrament of the Anointing of the Sick.

A priest came, hurriedly did some kind of ceremony that only took a few minutes and left. Hannah had never been present at an anointing of the sick before, but she felt uneasy, almost as though her father had not received 'the Last Rites'. She called another parish priest. When this priest arrived, he performed a lengthy ritual over her father which included something called 'The Commendation of the Dying' (not the *Condemnation* of the Dying', ha ha).

The Commendation comprises various biblical and deliverance prayers and litanies that recount 'from-death-to-life' Scripture passages.[4] Since her father was unconscious,

---

4. See http://www.ibreviary.com/m/preghiere.php?tipo=Rito&id=371 (last accessed 16 October 2017).

the priest wasn't able to administer Holy Communion, but he gave absolution and a final blessing.

After the sacrament, Hannah was about to rush back to the side of her father to hold his hand and comfort him as she had been doing, but the hospice nurses held her back. 'Wait,' they instructed, having seen this many times before; **'he's going to respond to the sacrament.'** 'What do you mean?' Hannah asked, confused.

'Your father is going to respond to the sacrament. Either he will take a turn for the better for a while, or he will be released.' Sure enough, her father's puckered brow and permanent look of consternation relaxed into a peaceful countenance. He drew one last enormous breath and exhaled every last bit of it as he died. Hannah was at once saddened, relieved and astonished.

The more I study St Pope John Paul II's *Theology of the Body,* the more I see how concrete our God is, what a materialist He is. (He must love matter because He made so much of it, and it's not going away. Rather, there will be a 'new heaven and a **new earth**,' Revelation 21).

John Paul II says in his *Theology of the Body* that

> the spousal meaning of the body is completed by the redemptive meaning on the different roads of life and in different situations: not only in marriage or... virginity,

celibacy, but also... in the many kinds of human suffering, indeed, in man's very birth and death. (TOB 102:8)

JP2 did not take up these last two themes in his masterwork, but others have built on it. For example, a new book is entitled *Theology of the Body, Extended: the Spiritual Signs of Birth, Impairment, and Dying*.

There can be so much fear surrounding the certain prospect of our own death. But we must trust in the One who loves us and Who accompanies us in the person of his priest, 'another Christ', administering the Sacraments at our major life-events: hatched, matched and dispatched.

It is said that the last words of Pope John Paul II were mumbled weakly in Polish, as he struggled to breathe and swallow: **'Let me go to the house of the Father.'** Six hours later, in a comatose state, the great Karol Wojtyla died.

Sr Helena Burns FSP, also known as the Media Nun, is a member of the Daughters of St Paul, an international congregation founded to communicate God's Word through the media. She is a speaker, author of *He Speaks to You*, and Catholic movie reviewer @ http://hellburns.blogspot.co.uk. Sr Helena has developed a Theology of the Body curriculum which she presents to teens, young adults and adults.

Witnessing the Power of Jesus to Heal

Fr Kevin Scallon CM

Michael, who worked at the seminary, asked me if I would call to see his next-door neighbour who had cancer. I said yes and he drove me to her home. She was a young married woman who had just returned from hospital. She had cancer of the throat, and the doctor sent her home to be with her family for the last few days of her life. Her husband was there, and their four children, a little girl with three older brothers. I told them who I was, and asked each of them their names.

They all stared at me with a mixture of hope and apprehension. My own heart was empty and I wondered what I could possibly do for this poor skeletal young mother. I have often had that feeling of emptiness in situations like that. I think the Lord allows me to feel this way so that I might realise who the real healer is. All my life, ever since I heard of the Sacrament of the Sick, I had an unusual sense of faith in its efficacy. It has always been a special feature of my ministry as a priest.

So I sat down with them and began to talk to them about why I was there.

'You know that I am a priest,' I said. 'I am here to make Jesus present to you because in the sacraments we meet Jesus himself.'

I looked at the children and said, 'Jesus can heal your mother. Do you believe this?'

'Yes, Father,' they said.

They were ready to believe anything. I told them that we read in the Gospels of how Jesus went about doing good and healing the sick.

'Well,' I said, 'He is still doing that in the sacraments of the Church, especially this Sacrament of the Anointing of the Sick and the Holy Eucharist.'

I explained how I would pray special prayers, lay my hands on their mother, anoint her with the Holy Oil of the Sick, and ask Jesus to heal her. They were all full of hope and sure faith that Jesus would come and care for their poor sick mother. It is always important that the priest gives a short teaching on the reality of the presence of Jesus in the sacrament. Very many people have little understanding of this. When I had finished, I assured them that I would continue to pray for their mother, and for all of them, especially during Holy Mass. I left and the visit faded into memory.

Thirty years later, while I was still at the seminary, a woman called to see me.

As often happens, she said, 'Do you remember me, Father?'

To which I honestly replied, 'I am sorry; I do not.'

'You came to see me thirty years ago when I was dying of cancer, and you prayed with me and anointed me in the Sacrament of the Sick.'

'Oh yes,' I replied, 'now I remember.'

'Well,' she said, 'from the moment you ministered to me, I immediately began to get better, and in a short time I was completely healed and restored to normal health, and I have never been sick since. I often intended to come to see you, but I never seemed to get around to it.' She stood there a picture of health, her husband at home, her children grown with families of their own.

I always encourage priests to minister this wonderful sacrament, no matter how busy they are at that moment. It is the healing ministry of Christ himself, and we must always provide him with the opportunity of easing the sufferings of the poor. I have witnessed the power of Jesus to heal every kind of sickness including depression, addictions, and an abundance of hidden ailments that even the wonderful skills of doctors of modern medicine could not reach. My expectation of this sacrament is that people will be healed, and not the opposite. It is my firm conviction that when we priests bring the healing Christ to people through this sacrament, our merciful Saviour always does something for them. But it is the presence of Christ himself, and the peace and fortitude that only He can impart, that makes the greatest difference in the lives of the poor and afflicted.

Fr Kevin J. Scallon CM is a priest of the Vincentian Community, international author and speaker who initially ministered in England and Nigeria. In 1976 he started the Intercession for Priests in Ireland and along with Sr Briege McKenna has travelled extensively around the world ministering to priests and lay people.

Conclusion

Sometimes when I pray with people, images and pictures come to mind. The images are almost like a plasma screen in my mind, where the picture/scene unfolds. I explain that St Paul talks about this in one of his letters about the gifts of the Holy Spirit (1 Corinthians 12:7-10).

For example, on one occasion I had been asked to visit a seriously ill patient in the hospital, and after he had gone to confession and received the Sacrament of the Anointing of the Sick, we prayed together. During this time of prayer, I received a couple of images; I said that if they meant anything to him he could meditate upon them, but if not, just let them go. At this point we had both been joined by his daughter. I described the first image: in it I saw him at the top of a snowy mountain, dressed as a mountaineer and I felt God was saying to him that He takes us to where we need to be. In the second image, he had an empty butterfly net and was trying to make a catch. I felt a strong sense he was meant to be open to discovering the beauty and wonder God had for him. This image, I believed, also represented new life for him (as that is what a butterfly does – brings new life from a caterpillar and cocoon state). After I shared these images he seemed deep in thought but his daughter was excited. She explained that her dad was a mountain climber (he had climbed three mountains) and that when she was a child they used to go butterfly-catching. The images resonated with them both and seemed to be a source of strength for the situation he was in.

God knows us so well, in the intimate details of our lives. He speaks his language of love into our hearts in a way we can best understand. There is not a single thing in our lives He does not want to be part of, reclaim and transform through his love. Everything matters to him because He seeks our holiness (Leviticus 20:26). Please never make the mistake I made by thinking you need to be good enough before you can go to him. He meets us in our brokenness and our vulnerability because He loves us so much. Holiness, as we have seen in this book, is surrendering our entire life to God, especially our weaknesses, and allowing him to transform us in His love. The more we give him, the more He transforms and the holier we become, just as St Paul explained, 'It is no longer I who live but Christ in me' (Galatians 2:20).

Our first vocation is to be holy, to show forth God's image to the world, by being transformed into the image of God's only Son, Jesus (CCC 1877). And this happens in a profound way through the sacraments. As we have read, the infusion, the outpouring of his divine life and love through the sacraments is meant to fill our souls and impact our lives in such a way that we can be the face of

Christ to our neighbour, bringing his love and healing to our families, neighbourhoods, nations, and out into the world. And don't forget, the deeper your union with Christ the more you share in the divine intimacy that the Son shares with the Father and Holy Spirit (CCC 850). But it is down to us – how open and receptive our hearts are to the sacraments – whether they will produce great fruit in our lives. Our faith, trust and openness is key! (CCC 1098, 2563).

I hope through reading this book you have been inspired by the testimonies of the contributors. And that if you did not already know, you do now, that God has amazing plans for you – through the sacraments that make us holy. He wants your soul to shimmer, to shine and to radiate his beauty out into the world.

Some of the stories in this book may have resonated with you. Or maybe it has not happened for you, but the testimonies in this book are inspiring you to embark on that journey… or maybe you feel you're not in a position to begin. But here's the thing: you're only one confession away from receiving an outpouring of this Divine love and life to set you on your way. Depending on your current lifestyle it may involve a radically brave decision to change your way of living for the sake of the Gospel and all that God wants to do in your life. After all, God wants you to be a **saint**!

But there are never any easy routes to such a high calling. To follow Christ is the way of the cross (Mark 8:34), but through that cross is eternal life. As St Rose of Lima put it, 'Apart from the cross there is no other ladder by which we may get to heaven.' But as we have seen in this book, despite the sacrifices and difficulties we undertake for God, He provides us with the deeply rooted love, joy, peace and strength to endure. That, no person, place or thing can take away from us.

May I make a suggestion? If you haven't yet experienced all that God wants you to have in the sacraments, let Our Lady help you. She was a great source of strength for me when I felt I was just not good enough to approach God. She brought me to him. Over the years I have received so much grace from God through her intercession. As your spiritual mother (John 19:27) she wants to assist and lead you to encounters with her Son. When the angel Gabriel appeared to her he announced she was full of grace (Luke 1:28): not half-full, a little bit of grace, but full of grace. She knew what it was to overflow with the love of God, to be holy. As the Immaculate Conception, through the Incarnation, at Pentecost, she accompanied the disciples and apostles by helping to prepare them to receive the Holy Spirit. She would have helped them understand and comprehend the Holy Spirit's fullness, as one who already knew the intimacy and love of the Father. If she was there for them, she will be there for you, if you invite her.

A big heartfelt thanks to all the contributors of this book: all those who have written, shared or contributed testimonies to help bring you into a deeper personal relationship with God through his life-giving sacraments, lived out in love and service to him and your neighbour.

And never forget, you're only ever a few decisions away from being the person God wants you to be – so you're only ever a few decisions away from being a saint!

As St Catherine of Siena says:

If you are what you are meant to be, you will set the whole world on fire!

Chapter Collaborators

Barbara Reed Mason (USA) is an evangelist, catechist, artist and author who has been involved in faith formation for over 25 years. In the UK and internationally, Barbara gives retreats, talks, Bible studies and courses in the faith. She is the author of the *Kerygma Bible Retreat* and the study guide *Is Religion Necessary? And Other Questions.* She has played a significant role in this book being produced.

Fr Julian Green (UK) is a priest of the Archdiocese of Birmingham currently serving in three parishes in Stoke-on-Trent. He was formerly a Catholic Chaplain to the University of Birmingham and Seminary Lecturer at Oscott College (Birmingham) specialising in Ecclesiology and Mariology. He is a member of the Society of St John Vianney.

Charlotte Hibbert (UK) is a Lay Chaplain at St Bede's College Manchester, and Young Adults Coordinator for the Reignite project in Salford Diocese. Charlotte is an experienced speaker and workshop leader and with her husband Christopher delivers marriage preparation courses within the diocese. Recently they have both been involved in the promotion of 'Family Is Sacred' by the Catholic

Bishops of England and Wales. Charlotte and Christopher have three children.

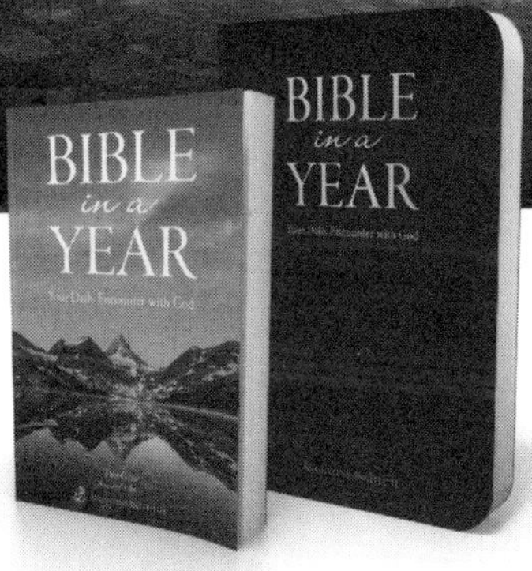

6